INDIA

Radhika Srinivasan/Leslie Jermyn

BENCHMARK BOOKS

MARSHALL CAVENDISH
NEW YORK

PICTURE CREDITS

A. Grinsted, Bes Stock, Diane Wilson, Fotomedia, Hulton-Deutsch, Image Bank, Indian High Commission of Singapore, Indian Tourist Bureau of Singapore, Jane Duff, Joanna van Gruisen, Jon Burbank, Joginder Chawla, Libby Howells, Neil Beer, Nirmal Ghosh, Ng Toon Juan, Photobank, Radhika Srinivasan, Raghu Rai, Richard I'Anson, Sheila Brown, Susanna Burton, Sylvia Cordaiy Photo Library, The Straits Times, Trip Photographic Library, Veronique Sanson

ACKNOWLEDGMENTS

Thanks to Jai Kasturi, Middle Eastern and Asian Languages and Cultures Department, Columbia University, for his expert reading of this manuscript

PRECEDING PAGE

Indian women playing traditional Indian string instruments.

Marshall Cavendish Benchmark
99 White Plains Road
Tarrytown, NY 10591
Web site: www.marshallcavendish.us

Originated and designed by Times Books International
An imprint of Marshall Cavendish International (Asia) Private Limited
A member of Times Publishing Limited

Library of Congress Cataloging-in-Publication Data
Srinivasan, Radhika.
India / Radhika Srinivasan.
   p. cm. — (Cultures of the world)
Includes bibliographical references and index.
   ISBN 0-7614-1354-5
1. India—Juvenile literature [1. India.] I. Title. II. Series.
DS407 .S74 2001
954—dc21   2001028608

Printed in Malaysia

10 9 8 7 6

CONTENTS

Feeding the rats of Rajasthan.

The earth tones of this family's house contrast sharply with the vivid colors of their clothing.

INTRODUCTION

INDIA IS REMARKABLE FOR ITS DIVERSITY, both cultural and geographical. It is home to several ethnic groups, each with its own language and culture. The separate histories of these groups are, however, woven together in a tapestry that depicts the origins of some of the world's major religions—such as Buddhism and Hinduism—and the spread of others—such as Islam and Christianity. This variety of cultures and religions is reflected in the vibrancy and color of Indian music, dance, and festivals and in the architectural styles of the country's majestic palaces and temples.

In geographical terms, India is the world's seventh largest country. It boasts contrasting landscapes—high mountains and low river plains, deserts and tropical jungles—and a diversity of animals and plants that rivals the diversity of the people. With more than a billion people, India faces the challenges of providing everyone with an adequate living and of preserving nature's bounty. Read on to discover more about this fascinating subcontinent.

GEOGRAPHY

INDIA IS ABOUT ONE-THIRD THE SIZE of the United States of America. With an area of 1.27 million square miles (3.3 million square km), it is the seventh largest country in the world. It is a subcontinent bounded by the Himalayas in the north and vast seas in the south. To the east is the Bay of Bengal, and to the west, the Arabian Sea. Both these bodies of water stretch southward to join the Indian Ocean.

The Himalayan mountain range—one of the longest mountain chains in the world—extends over a distance of 1,490 miles (2,398 km) from the northern state of Jammu and Kashmir (which India and Pakistan both claim) to the eastern border state of Arunachal Pradesh. Within the Himalayas is the world's highest peak, Everest.

At either end of the Himalayas are more mountain ranges. A few passes provide crossing points. The Khyber and Bolan passes in the northwest (now in Pakistan) are particularly significant, having served as entry points for several groups of foreign invaders, who marched into India in the course of its long and eventful history.

Nepal and China are India's northern neighbors; Afghanistan and Pakistan are situated in the northwest; and Myanmar (Burma) and Bangladesh are located in the east. Sri Lanka lies to the south, barely an hour's boat ride from the subcontinent's southern tip. In the southeast, close to Indonesia, are India's Andaman and Nicobar islands.

Below: **India's landscape also boasts beautiful water scenes. Here, two boys stand on a boulder amid the waters that flow from the Dudhsagar falls —the highest in India— located in Goa.**

Opposite: **India's roof— the Ladakh plateau of Kashmir.**

MOUNTAINS AND RIVERS

India can be divided roughly into three geographical regions: the mountainous Himalayan north, the fertile Gangetic Plain, and the rocky Deccan south. The Himalayas are the source of three of India's major rivers—the Indus, the Ganges, and the Brahmaputra. The Indus flows mostly into Pakistan, while the Brahmaputra flows into Bangladesh, before reaching the Bay of Bengal. The Ganges, which Indians consider the holiest of rivers, flows from the Himalayas, through the states of Uttar Pradesh, Bihar, and West Bengal, and into the Ganges Delta, before draining into the Bay of Bengal.

While the rivers in the north are snow-fed, most of the rivers in the south are rain-fed and fluctuate in volume. The Godavari, Krishna, Mahanadi, and Cauvery rivers enrich the soil in the southern region. The Gangetic Plain, fed by the Ganges River's abundant water supply, has rich alluvial soil and is one of the most fertile and densely populated tracts of land in the world. The triangular region south of the Gangetic Plain consists mainly of the rocky, uneven Deccan Plateau. Bordering this plateau on either side are smaller mountains, known as the Eastern and Western Ghats.

The Vindhya Mountains and the Narmada River stretch across the central area of the subcontinent, separating the north from the south. The presence of

Bathing in the holy waters of the Ganges River.

these two geographical features are a big reason why the histories of the north and south have often taken different courses.

This physical division probably also accounts for the different languages Indians speak today. There are two language families in the country: the languages of the north—Hindi, Punjabi, Gujarati, and Rajasthani, for example—are generally descended from Sanskrit and are part of the Indo-European language family; the languages of the south—Tamil, Telugu, Kannada, and Malayalam, for example—are part of the Dravidian language family.

Although India has a long coastline, it has few natural harbors. Changing sea levels in the past have shifted the country's coastline, and as a result, ancient ports, such as Tamluk in the east, Kaveripatnam in the south, and Lothal in the west, are today landlocked.

A camel caravan takes a break on its trek across the desert.

SEASONS AND CLIMATE

India's climate varies from torrid to arctic, depending on the region and the season. The country experiences six seasons: summer, autumn, winter, spring, summer monsoon, and winter monsoon. The northeast and southeast monsoon winds influence India's climate.

The valleys of Kashmir and Simla in the north of the country are delightfully cool in the summer months (April–June), but reach freezing temperatures in the winter months (December–January). New Delhi, also in the north, experiences thunderstorms preceded by dust storms in July and August.

In contrast, the central and southern regions of India experience largely tropical weather. For Mumbai and the Western Ghats, June to September are wet months, when annual rainfall reaches 118 inches (3,000 mm). Chennai and places farther south get more rain in December. In the hot season, the weather can be oppressive, with temperatures rising as high as 122°F (50°C) in central India.

Wild mustard plants in bloom—a sign of spring.

Rainfall also varies from region to region. In the eastern state of Assam, near the Khasi Hills, annual rainfall can be as high as 430 inches (10,920 mm). Cherrapunji in the east holds world records for the most rain received both in a year and in a month—1,042 inches (26,461 mm) and 366 inches (9,300 mm) respectively.

Occasionally, a shortage of rain leads to drought and famine, while excessive rain causes flash floods and the loss of lives. In an agricultural country such as India, the farmers are at the mercy of the weather. For this reason, Indian farmers often pray to the rain god, Varuna, either to protect them from floods or to bless them with abundant rain.

NATURAL RESOURCES

India's varied climate supports a rich range of vegetation. The Himalayan region is wooded with pines and conifers, while eastern India has luxuriant forests and thick clumps of bamboo. The subcontinent boasts some 1,606 million acres (6.5 million square km) of forests and 45,000 plant species, many not found anywhere else in the world. There are several protected reserves, but trees are still being felled for fuel.

India is also blessed with a wide variety of mineral deposits, including iron ore, coal, lignite, silver, copper, gold, and zinc. Coal and lignite provide for more than 60 percent of India's energy consumption; wood, oil, and natural gas provide for much of the rest, making the subcontinent almost completely self-sufficient in meeting its energy needs.

Lumber firms operate outside protected areas to exploit India's rich timber resources.

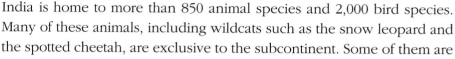
WILDLIFE

Top: **An Indian elephant.**

Bottom: **A female rhinoceros caressing her baby.**

India is home to more than 850 animal species and 2,000 bird species. Many of these animals, including wildcats such as the snow leopard and the spotted cheetah, are exclusive to the subcontinent. Some of them are endangered, and there are no fewer than 63 national parks and 350 sanctuaries to protect these animals.

The Indian elephant is well known for its friendliness towards humans and for its role in temple and palace ceremonies. So common are wild elephants in the Mudumalai sanctuary in the south and in the Assam forests in the east, that they sometimes stray into houses and trample gardens! Elephant killing and the sale of ivory have been outlawed in almost every country in the world. Yet sadly, many of these majestic creatures are still hunted for their tusks, which fetch a fabulous price on the black market.

The bison, buffalo, black buck, and nilgai (a type of antelope) are some other animals commonly seen in India. Rhinoceroses, jackals, and monkeys of different kinds are also found in the jungles of central India.

The birds that inhabit the subcontinent range from tiny sunbirds, no bigger than butterflies, to cranes and vultures. Wild peacocks, brilliantly colored pheasants, and fowls abound in the northern state of Rajasthan, where one can also see migratory Siberian cranes flying south to nest in December or January.

POPULATION

An official population census is taken once every 10 years in India. The 1991 census put the total population at 844.3 million. This number rose above the one billion mark in 1999 and reached 1,027,015,247 in March 2001. India is only the second country in the world, after China, to have grown to more than one billion people.

Overpopulation is a major problem in a country where half the adults are illiterate, more than half the children are undernourished, and a third of the population lives in poverty. Growing by 18 million people every year, India is expected to overtake China as the most populous country in the world before 2050.

More than 70 percent of India's population is in farming. Many of them have little or no formal education and live in large families of five to six children. In contrast, most urban families are nuclear, with two to three children.

The cities face urbanization problems. According to current estimates, Mumbai is the largest Indian city, with a population of 18 million. Each day, thousands of people enter Mumbai in search of work. New Delhi, Calcutta, Chennai, and Bangalore are other overpopulated cities.

While cities like Mumbai and Calcutta boast the luxurious mansions of movie stars and businesspeople, they also have thousands of very poor and ill-fed people living in shanty slums and on sidewalks.

Indians assembled at the India Gate grounds in New Delhi.

HISTORY

INDIA'S PAST IS STRONGLY LINKED to the Indus River, which flows about 1,700 miles (2,736 km) from the Himalayan Mountains to the Arabian Sea. The Indians called the river Sindhu; the Persians referred to it as the Hindu. But it was the Greeks who gave the river and the land around it their present name—Indus.

India's history goes back more than 5,000 years. In 1924, the ancient cities of Mohenjo-Daro and Harappa were discovered in what is Pakistan today. Two ancient sites in India are Ropar in Punjab and Kalilbangan in Rajasthan, along the Indus. Indications of an advanced civilization dating back from around 2500 B.C. have been found, such as brick houses, a well-planned drainage system, and script-bearing clay seals. Historians speculate that nomadic peoples settled along the river plain, perhaps imitating the success of earlier farming communities. The cycle of the Indus was crucial, for as the waters receded each summer, the rich alluvial soil left behind was eminently suitable for agriculture. How this farming lifestyle evolved into a sophisticated culture remains a mystery.

Historians in the 19th century theorized that the people of the Indus Valley were Dravidians and that Aryans (Indo-Europeans, possibly from Iran) came to the subcontinent around 1500 B.C. and mingled with the prevailing people. Due to a lack of direct evidence, however, many scholars today question this theory.

During the Vedic period, the four *Vedas* ("vay-dahs")—Books of Knowledge—were written (*veda* is the Sanskrit word for "knowledge"). The *Vedas* contain hymns that address primarily the origin of life and the glorification of nature, personified as *devas* ("day-vahs"), or gods, such as Agni and Varuna, the gods of fire and rain respectively. These gods were worshiped with rituals, sacrifices, and the recitation of the hymns, which priests today still chant during Hindu ceremonies in homes and temples.

Opposite: **Carved images of the gods cover the walls of the ancient Hindu Samnath Pur temple in Mysore.**

BUDDHA

Prince Siddhartha was born in 563 B.C. at Kapilavastu in Nepal. He lived in luxury, married at 16, and had a son. One day, setting out from his palace, the prince saw a feeble old man. The next day, he saw a sick man, and the third day, he saw a corpse being taken for cremation. It was the prince's first experience of illness and death.

So moved by pain was the prince that he renounced everything and went in search of answers to his questions on the cause of human misery.

After a period of meditation, he received a vision of enlightenment and came to be known as *Buddha*, "the one who knows."

BIRTH OF RELIGIONS

The ruling classes believed they were nobler than the laboring masses who cultivated the land. They divided society into four social classes, based on occupation: Brahmin ("BRAH-min"), the priestly class; Kshatriya ("SHAH-tree-yah"), the ruling class; Vaisya ("VY-shee-yah"), the merchant class; and Sudra ("SOOD-rah"), the laboring class.

Gradually these class distinctions transformed into a broad system, in which social, economic, and religious status became semihereditary and interacted in complex ways.

The post-Vedic period saw the birth of many Sanskrit works, such as the *Puranas* ("poo-RAH-nahs")—Old World Legends—and epic tales, such as the *Ramayana* ("reh-MAH-yah-nah") and the *Mahabharata* ("mah-hah-BHAH-reh-tah").

Rituals and animal sacrifices increased, in the belief that the gods could be appeased by them. And two great religious thinkers were born: Vardhamana Mahavira, the founder of Jainism, and Siddharta Gautama, the founder of Buddhism.

THE GREEK GIFT AND KING ASOKA

In 327 B.C., Alexander the Great, the Greek Macedonian invader, conquered the Persian Empire and marched into northwestern India as far as the river Beas in Punjab. Although Alexander's victory was temporary and had little long-term political impact, the contact led to an exchange of ideas between India and the West for the first time.

In the northwestern regions, Greek sculpture provided the model for Indian gods and goddesses. Almost 500 years after Buddha's death, images of this man-turned-god were created, first with Greek features and later in distinctly Indian styles. The Greek and Indian art forms became famous at two Buddhist centers, Gandhara and Mathura. Greek influence is therefore a landmark in the history of Indian art.

Politically, at this time, India was divided into many states, each ruled by a prince. The first king to unite the princely states and promote Buddhism both within and outside India was King Asoka (reigned 272–232 B.C.) of the Mauryan Dynasty.

Asoka's war with the Kalinga kingdom (spanning Orissa and the region to its south) proved a turning point in his life. The excessive bloodshed at the battle shocked his conscience. Almost overnight, he became a Buddhist, spreading the message of peace and nonviolence. He inscribed Buddhist principles of morality on rocks and pillars and spent the remainder of his life performing acts of charity, helping the poor and the needy.

Buddhism spread to Sri Lanka, Central Asia, and Afghanistan, thanks to Asoka's zeal. The Asoka pillar, now in the New Delhi museum, is crowned with a four-headed lion and a *chakra* ("chah-krah"), or wheel, at the center. This is India's national emblem today, signifying spiritual fearlessness and diligence.

Opposite top: **A stone sculpture of the Buddha.**

Opposite bottom: **Mahavira, the founder of Jainism.**

Below: **The four-headed lion of the *Asokachakra*, India's national symbol.**

Opposite: **This detail of a fresco in the caves at Ajanta is believed to represent a prince.**

GOLDEN AGE OF THE GUPTAS

After the fall of the Mauryan Empire, much of northern India became disunited and fell into the hands of foreign powers—the Persians, Huns, Scythians, and Sakas from Central Asia. Of these invaders, a people known as the Yueh Chi advanced upon the northwestern frontiers and brought parts of China, Central Asia, Afghanistan, and northern India under a single rule. Kanishka, the Yueh Chi king, is remembered chiefly for his role in taking Buddhism into the remote corners of Asia. He started the Saka era, which for a full thousand years was used as a standard for dates throughout Asia, just as the Christian era is used today as the standard for dates throughout much of the world.

After a gap of more than two centuries in political history, the strong Gupta Dynasty took over India and gave the country a long period of peace and prosperity. Chandra Gupta Vikramaditya (A.D. 380–413), the best known Gupta king, was a great patron of art and literature. The poet and dramatist Kalidasa—the "Indian Shakespeare" born 12 centuries before the English bard—and the physician Charaka graced Vikramaditya's court. Kalidasa is considered the greatest figure in classical Sanskrit literature. Aryabhata, the mathematician who discovered the laws governing *shunya* ("SHOON-yah"), or zero, and who explained the method of calculating eclipses, also came from this golden age of the Guptas.

Many great Hindu temples and Buddhist monasteries were built in the golden age of the Guptas. Of these, the 29 Ajanta Caves in central India are the most outstanding. Carved out of solid rock, the walls and ceilings depict scenes from Buddha's life. Ajanta Caves' paintings provided the inspiration for the Dun Huang caves in China, the Horyu temple in Japan, and Buddhist cave paintings in Central Asia.

SOUTHERN INDIA

Since ancient times, southern India has enjoyed greater peace and stability than northern India. Tamil was and still is the language of the south. In fact, it is the oldest living language in the world today.

Of the Tamil rulers, the Pallavas and Cholas have left a lasting imprint on southern India. The Pallavas built the rock-cut shore temple at Mamallapuram near Madras and reestablished the worship of Shiva and Vishnu. Shiva and Vishnu are the Hindu gods of destruction and preservation, respectively.

The Cholas are remembered for the magnificently constructed Hindu temples and bronze sculptures found in Tanjore, Kanchi, and Chidambaram. They also promoted music, dance, and learning throughout their united southern empire.

The Chola Empire extended as far south as Sri Lanka for a while, under King Rajendra Chola (reigned A.D.1014–1044). Chola also established trade links with China via Southeast Asia. Indian culture spread to most parts of Southeast Asia from the beginning of the fourth century A.D., but especially during Chola rule, between the eighth and 11th centuries. Buddhist monasteries and Hindu temples in Java, Sumatra, Malaya, Thailand, and Cambodia reveal a strong Indian influence. Their language, literature, art, and political systems are also inspired by Indian models.

From the fourth to ninth centuries, southern India was the birthplace of many Tamil poet-saints, who revived the people's faith in Hindu gods and goddesses. In addition to writing poems in praise of Vishnu and Shiva, these poet-saints rejuvenated Hindu religious practices among Jain and Buddhist kings. The Alwars and Nayanmars, as these poet-saints were called, were pioneers of a Hindu revivalist movement that eventually swept all of India. They are still revered today in southern India.

Mamallapuram, the rock-cut shore temple in Tamil Nadu. Mamallapuram was the seventh-century port city of the Pallavas and was named after King Mamalla.

MEDIEVAL INDIA

While southern India continued to enjoy considerable peace, northern India experienced several invasions after the ninth century. The kings of the northern Indian kingdoms remained divided and weak and could not resist Muslim attacks.

Arabs, Turks, Afghans, and Mongols made successive inroads into northern and western India. They plundered Hindu and Buddhist places of worship, removing vast treasures of gold and jewelry. Worst of all the looting was the sacking of the famous Somnatha temple in 1026 by Mahmud of Ghazni, who escaped with a huge amount of the temple's wealth of gold and jewels.

The only real resistance came from the proud Rajput warriors of western India. There are many tales relating the courage of Rajput women, who preferred to burn themselves alive rather than surrender to the Muslim invaders. But even the fierce Rajputs could not withstand the Muslim attacks.

It was not until the 13th century that the Muslim invaders settled down and formed a stable government. Out of political chaos rose a half-Mongol, half-Turk named Babur, whose grandson Akbar established the Mughal Empire in India.

The Taj Mahal in Agra, built by Mughal Emperor Shah Jahan as a mausoleum for his beloved wife Mumtaz Mahal, has been hailed as "marbled embroidery" for its intricate workmanship.

MUGHAL SPLENDOR

Akbar the Great was the first Mughal king to extend his empire to cover the whole of northern and central India. He married a Rajput princess, showed great tolerance toward Hindus, and initiated a fusion of Hindu and Muslim art forms in architecture, painting, music, and dance.

Akbar (1542–1605) built the splendid city of Fatehpur Sikri near Delhi. It had a hall called Ibadad Khana, in which people gathered to discuss various religious doctrines. Akbar dreamed of founding a world faith called the Din-i-Ilahi, or religion of the world. His son, Jahangir (reigned 1605–1627), was fond of landscaping Mughal gardens into replicas of a Persian paradise. Some of these gardens can still be seen in Udaipur and Kashmir. Jahangir also loved painting, and this led to the growth of many schools of miniature painting in India.

Jahangir's son, Shah Jahan (c. 1592–1666), is well remembered for the forts and mosques he constructed at enormous cost. The most outstanding is the marble mausoleum, Taj Mahal, built in loving memory of his queen, Mumtaz Mahal. It took 22,000 workmen 22 years to finish building the Taj Mahal, complete with gates of solid silver at the main entrance and precious gems and stones inlaid throughout the entire structure.

With the exception of Aurangzeb (1618–1707), Shah Jahan's son, the Mughal kings were great lovers of music. North Indian classical dance and music—once religious—became secular, having entered the Mughal courts. The North Indian style became distinctly romantic, with the introduction of elements of Urdu poetry.

However, the people became poorer, especially during the cruel reign of Aurangzeb. Heavy taxes and temple funds filled the royal treasury. Landless laborers and manual workers became bonded slaves, and crime increased in the countryside.

ARRIVAL OF THE EUROPEANS

Politically, the 17th century proved ripe for yet another foreign power to enter India—the British. In 1600, Queen Elizabeth I granted a royal charter to a group of English traders to set up a trading company, the East India Company, in the East. With a small fleet under the leadership of William Hawkins, they set up trading posts in Bombay (now Mumbai), Madras, and Calcutta. The French, Dutch, and Portuguese established their own trading centers, buying textiles, tea, spices, gold, and silver cheaply in India and selling their purchases at an enormous profit in Europe. The European trading stations grew into flourishing cities.

The British East India Company signed treaties with various Indian *maharajas* ("mah-hah-RAH-jahs"), or princes, who gave the British economic advantage and political power. The fall of the Mughal Empire, the divisiveness of the Indian kings, and the enterprising shrewdness of the British backed with military might paved the way for a British empire in India in the 18th century.

"If anywhere on Earth there is paradise, it is here, it is here, it is here."

—Jahangir, a Mughal emperor, on his visit to the Valley of Kashmir in the early 1600s.

Swami Vivekananda

Raja Ram Mohun Roy

BRITISH INDIA

Numerous small mutinies eventually culminated in the Sepoy Revolt of 1857. The British had introduced new rifles loaded with lubricated cartridges, the ends of which had to be bitten off before use. This offended the Hindu and Muslim soldiers, because the lubricant contained animal fat. To the former, cows were sacred; to the latter, eating pork was forbidden. This was the final straw in a decade of discontent over the mistreatment of Indian soldiers by the British East India Company.

But the rebellion was put down, and the British Crown took over the government of India, making India a British colony. The British introduced modern technology to manufacture goods, such as textiles and machines. They built railways to facilitate administration, established factories, schools, and universities, and introduced the Western concept of democracy. They also encouraged missionary activity and the spread of Christianity.

MODERN INDIA

At the start of the 20th century, some liberal British policies brought social and economic reforms. The British initiated constitutional changes and local self-government at the village level and recognized the newly formed

EARLY REFORM MOVEMENTS

The 19th century saw the growth of many political, social, and religious reform movements. Raja Ram Mohan Roy started the Brahmo Samaj in 1828 to fight social ills such as the caste system, child marriage, superstitions, and *sati* ("sah-tee")—the burning of widows. Ramakrishna Paramahamsa, a Hindu mystic, preached that true worship of God lies in the service of humanity. His disciple, Swami Vivekananda, established a Hindu order called the Ramakrishna Mission and awakened the conscience of Indians.

24

political party, the Indian National Congress. English education created Indian intellectuals who craved India's freedom.

At this time, Mohandas Karamchand Gandhi (1869–1948) was becoming a household name in India. Born in South Africa, Gandhi—better known by his title of Mahatma, meaning "great soul"—came to India and gave up his law practice to fight for India's independence. He advocated *satyagraha* ("SEHT-yah-grah-hah"), the nonviolent fight for justice.

Gandhi advocated peaceful strikes. He persuaded his followers to wear Indian handloom textiles instead of English cloth. He walked hundreds of miles in silent protest against the British tax on salt, forcing the removal of the tax. Gandhi's nonviolent strategy made British attempts to subjugate the resistance through military might almost impossible.

The British gave in, and India gained independence on August 15, 1947. Jawaharlal Nehru (1889–1964) became India's first prime minister. However, because Hindu and Muslim leaders could not overcome their differences, India was partitioned, and Pakistan was born. The Partition resulted in the world's largest mass movement of people and over a million deaths, as Hindus and Muslims murdered each other.

This monument, showing Mahatma Gandhi (far left) on one of his nonviolent protest marches, was built in honor of the man known affectionately as the "Father of the Nation." Gandhi was assassinated in 1948, not long after India's independence.

GOVERNMENT

INDIA BECAME A SOCIALIST DEMOCRATIC REPUBLIC on January 26, 1950. The country has a parliamentary system of government. Its states and union territories are governed by the Central Cabinet according to the Constitution adopted in 1950. Each state has its own government, but the union territories come under the government of the Central Cabinet.

The president, elected for a period of five years by members of parliament and state legislative assemblies, is the head of state and the constitutional head of the executive, legislative, and judicial branches of government. The president is also the commander of the Armed Forces— a ceremonial post—and acts on the advice of the Central Cabinet.

The Central Cabinet is headed by the prime minister. The real powers lie with this executive body. The Central Cabinet is responsible to the House of the People, or the Lok Sabha. Elections to the Lok Sabha are held every five years.

Legislative powers are the domain of the parliament—consisting of the Lok Sabha and the Rajya Sabha (Council of States)—which acts as a forum of public opinion. The judicial branch protects the constitutional and statutory rights of Indians.

The executive, legislative, and judicial branches work together to prevent the misuse of power. For example, the judicial arm aims to guard against the executive branch assuming powers beyond those outlined in the Constitution.

Below: **The Parliament House in New Delhi.**

Opposite: **A quick shine just before the parade.**

Dancers in Punjabi dress at a Republic Day parade. On the eve of January 26, families camp out through the night to get a vantage point from which to view the parade.

THE FEDERAL SYSTEM OF GOVERNMENT

The Constitution of India provides for a federal system of government similar to that of the United States, with the federal government at the center and a similar structure in the states. This decentralizes power and permits easy administration.

Each state has its own governor as the constitutional head, the chief minister and his council to work as the state executive, and the elected members of the Legislative Assembly. While the federal government covers important areas such as defense, foreign affairs, and communications, the state is given autonomy in several areas, including agriculture, internal law and order, and public health. This power structure continues all the way down to the districts and villages.

In a similar manner, the hierarchy of the Supreme Court, High Courts, Subordinate Courts, and the *panchayats* ("PEHN-chah-yehts")—or district and village courts—helps to dispense justice at various levels. To ensure uniformity, the Constitution has allowed for a single system of courts to administer both national and state laws.

Since people of different religions live in India, the Constitution has set different personal laws to help solve problems relating to family matters, such as marriage, divorce, and succession. The Hindu Marriage Act, for instance, cannot be applied to Muslims, whose laws of marriage follow the Hanafi doctrines of Sunni law. Similarly, different acts apply to the Christians and Parsis.

"India is a geographical and an economic entity, a cultural unity amid diversity, a bundle of contradictions held together by strong but invisible threads."

—Jawaharlal Nehru, India's first prime minister.

Left: **Campaign posters are everywhere at general election time.**

Below: **Defending India's territorial waters—a naval exercise in the Indian Ocean.**

THE CONSTITUTION

Many of India's policies have been guided by its constitutional principles. The Constitution of India—based in part on the Constitution of the United States—guarantees equality before the law and equal protection under the law and prohibits discrimination on the basis of religion, race, caste, sex, or place of birth. It also guarantees basic rights such as freedom of speech, assembly, association, religion, movement, and residence and upholds the right to acquire property and to practice a profession or trade. In 1976, the Constitution was amended to include the fundamental duties of each citizen. These fundamental duties ensure that every citizen abides by the Constitution, defends the country in times of crisis, and promotes harmony among all regions and religions.

POLITICAL LEADERS

India's first prime minister, Jawaharlal Nehru, was a freedom fighter and a great statesman. He remained the unquestioned leader until his death in 1964. Representing the Congress Party, which had a majority in the state legislatures as well as in the federal parliament, Nehru pursued a policy of industrialization and steered India into the modern era. After a brief interval, his daughter, Indira Gandhi (1917–1984), was elected to the post of prime minister. By this time, other national parties had grown to contend for leadership: the Congress Party split into two factions, and several parties had made their presence felt at the state level.

Indira Gandhi was generally popular, but some of her policies provoked outrage among certain groups of Indians. In 1975, she declared a state of emergency and suspended constitutional rights for 19 months. She was subsequently defeated in the 1977 elections but was re-elected within two years due to the lack of strong competition. In June 1984, Indira Gandhi sent the military into the Golden Temple at Amritsar—the Sikhs' most sacred temple—to flush out separatists. This ultimately led to her death: she was assassinated by her own Sikh bodyguard on October 31, 1984. Her son, Rajiv Gandhi, was elected prime minister by an overwhelming majority in December 1984, but his popularity waned rapidly amid allegations of corruption and the failure of several of his policies. In the 1989 elections, an opposition member, V.P. Singh, was elected prime minister, but he resigned in November 1990 following a no-confidence vote.

On May 21, 1991, during the election campaigns, Rajiv Gandhi was assassinated in Tamil Nadu. His party still won the elections, and Narasimha Rao became prime minister until 1996. The next two years saw two new prime ministers. Atal Behari Vajpayee has been in office since 1998.

Jawaharlal Nehru.

ECONOMY

INDIA HAS A MIXED ECONOMY. State-owned industries and enterprises include transportation, mining, armaments, communications, electricity, power, and all major commercial and district banks. The private sector handles consumer products, textiles, and electronics, among others.

Opposite: **A magazine vendor.**

Successive five-year plans have helped the Indian economy to grow steadily since the inception of the First Plan in 1951. The Ninth Plan covers the years from 1997 to 2002. Estimates put India's 1999–2000 growth rate at 5.9 percent, even though the agriculture sector—very important in a largely rural country—declined by 0.8 percent.

Growth in the contributions to the gross domestic product by the manufacturing and construction sectors was estimated at 7 percent and 9 percent respectively, up from 3.6 percent and 5.7 percent in 1998–99. At the same time, inflation dropped to international levels of 2–3 percent for the first time in decades.

INFRASTRUCTURE, MONEY, AND TRADE

A wide network of railways and roads links all of India's regions, while a vast number of cargo carriers passes through the country's ports. The two national airlines, Indian Airlines and Air India, help to maintain domestic and foreign air transportation services.

India's currency unit is the rupee. Approximately 46 rupees equaled US$1 on February 20, 2001. The Reserve Bank of India operates as the central bank, issuing notes and controlling the mint. India's foreign exchange reserves rose by more than US$2.4 billion in 1999–2000.

Exports expanded by 13 percent in 1999–2000. India exports mainly agricultural produce, textiles, chemicals, leather goods, iron, steel, and precious stones. It imports mainly crude oil and petroleum products, machinery, fertilizers, and chemicals.

Above: **A bio-gas plant, which converts animal, industrial, and human waste into methane gas.**

Opposite top: **A water wheel. In rural India, bullocks are still used to draw water.**

Opposite bottom: **Dried fish is a popular consumer product in the coastal regions.**

ENERGY

Most of India's electricity is produced using coal and petroleum products. About 40 percent is generated by hydroelectric power, and 3 percent is generated by India's two nuclear power plants located at Kota in Mumbai and Kalpakkam in Chennai.

India produces methane from animal waste, industrial discharge, and domestic sewage. These waste byproducts are recycled even further into enriched fertilizer. About 62,000 bio-gas units have been installed, since the All-India Coordinated Bio-gas Programme started in 1975.

In line with its conservation policy, India is tapping into the sun's energy to provide solar lighting for houses and solar-powered drinking water systems. Solar power stations are being built in rural areas.

About 70 percent of India's energy needs are met through indigenous production. However, India still imports petroleum products for its growing energy needs, mainly from oil-producing countries of the Middle East, including Iran, Iraq, and Saudi Arabia.

AGRICULTURE

India is primarily an agricultural country, with 70 percent of the population engaged in farming and 40 percent of the annual national product coming from agricultural goods. India is self-sufficient in rice and wheat.

Although farmers in some parts of India still use the antiquated bullock-drawn plow, many have made the transition to modern farming methods, using tractors, mechanized watering equipment, and pesticides and fertilizers. This has greatly increased grain production over the years.

However, India continues to import sugar, oils, and other commodities, as its own production is insufficient to meet domestic demand.

MINING AND MANUFACTURING

India ranks among the leading producers of iron ore, coal, and bauxite and is a significant producer of copper, mica, asbestos, chromium, gold, and silver. Cotton textiles head the list of manufactured items, with jute products next in importance.

Other important Indian industries are tea-processing, petroleum refining, sugar, silks and woolens, leather products, vegetable oils, paper, and the manufacture of electronic goods. Many consumer items are locally manufactured, including electrical goods, motor vehicles, television sets, video recorders, and computers. India's computer software is gaining popularity in the West.

ENVIRONMENT

INDIA IS HOME TO MANY PLANTS AND ANIMALS. It is not easy to balance the needs of the huge human population against the needs of nature. The Indian people and their government have made a strong commitment to preserving the subcontinent's natural treasures.

INDIA'S NATURAL DIVERSITY

India's varied landscapes form distinct ecological zones with unique flora and fauna. Tropical rain forests flourish in the northeastern parts of the subcontinent; thorn forests grow in Gujarat and Rajasthan; and tropical deciduous and dry alpine forests cover the Himalayan foothills. Mangrove forests line the coasts. Living in these habitats are 350 mammal species, 408 types of reptile, 1,224 bird species, 197 amphibian species, 2,546 varieties of fish, and about 15,000 flowering plants.

Today, however, some 193 animal species in India are either threatened or endangered. Despite the country's history of environmentalism and its cultural heritage of respect for living things, human development trends have created conflicts between the people and the wildlife. The government has passed laws in a bid to protect the environment.

Below: **Pine trees in Kashmir.**

Opposite: **Indian women in a field of sunflowers.**

ENDANGERED MAMMALS

THE ASIATIC LION Asiatic lions look much like their larger African cousins, except for their slightly shaggier mane and larger tail tuft. Asiatic lions once lived in an area that stretched across Southwest Asia from northern Greece to central India, but extensive hunting in the last century has severely depleted their numbers worldwide. Today their only natural habitat is the Gir Forest Sanctuary in the Indian state of Gujarat. Their population has grown steadily to over 240, since India banned lion hunting in the 1950s.

Yet even in their last home in the Gir Forest Sanctuary, the world's last Asiatic lions live an uneasy existence. They share their home with native herdsmen and tehir cattle. These herdsmen destroy the forest, when they fell trees for fuel and timber. They also kill lions to protect their cattle, the lions' alternative food source when natural prey such as deer are hard to find. Lions generally avoid contact with people, but they occasionally attack people when provoked or injured.

There are now laws protecting the Asiatic lion and plans to set up a second reserve for it. Helping the lion population regenerate is a mammoth task. The Delhi zoo's lion-breeding program initiated in 1959 welcomed its first lion cub only in 2000.

A female Asiatic lion.

Endangered mammals

THE TIGER Before 1900, India had between 80,000 and 100,000 tigers. Hunted for their skin and other body parts, these tigers dwindled in number to around 40,000 before 1947 and 1,800 before 1971. A conservation program called "Project Tiger" was then launched, which succeeded at least in reversing the tiger's path toward extinction. Today the tiger population in India has rebounded to 4,300, but the species is still on the endangered list.

THE SLOTH BEAR This nocturnal bear weighs from 175–310 pounds (79–141 kg). It has a coat of black and brown fur with white fur across the chest and on the face. Its mobile snout is ideal for sucking up termites, its main food. The sloth bear inhabits the forested areas south of the Himalayas. It is also found in Sri Lanka, Bhutan, and Bangladesh. It is protected by Indian law, but the main threat to its survival is the destruction of forests caused by logging and agriculture.

THE PYGMY HOG This is the smallest species of pig in the world, weighing only 13–22 pounds (6–10 kg). It was once thought to be extinct in India but was rediscovered in Assam in 1971. The pig lost a lot of its grasslands habitat to cattle grazing and human harvesting of thatch for houses. A very small pygmy hog population now lives in two Indian wildlife sanctuaries: Barnadi and Manas.

GANGES RIVER DOLPHIN This freshwater dolphin lives in the Ganges, Brahmaputra, Karnaphuli, and Meghana rivers. Water pollution and dam projects have reduced India's once thriving dolphin population to between 3,000 and 4,000. Because the dolphins migrate seasonally, it is difficult to set up sanctuaries for them. Further study is thus needed to come up with a way to protect this unique animal.

"It shall be the duty of every citizen of India ... to protect and improve the natural environment including forests, lakes, rivers and wildlife, and to have compassion for living creatures."

— Article 51A of the Indian Constitution.

ENVIRONMENTAL THREATS

SETTLEMENT The natural environment suffers wherever there is human activity. As populations grow and people have to look for new places to set up home, virgin forests are cleared to make way for buildings and roads, and land and marine resources are gradually drained to provide food and other materials for the human settlers.

The Indian people are largely rural and depend on farming for survival. As they look for land to plant food crops and rear animals, they take more and more space from animals, the land's original inhabitants. Some wild animal species have stopped breeding because of human interference. Others, like the Asiatic wild ass and the Gaur (Indian bison), contract diseases from domesticated horses and cattle. Still others, like the tiger and the Asiatic lion, are killed when they prey on livestock.

Human settlement carved into the land.

POACHING Many animals are hunted for their skins and body parts. Poachers have killed the Indian rhinocerous for its horn, the Asian elephant for its tusks, and the tiger and snow leopard for their pelts. Some of the body parts of the Asiatic black bear and the sloth bear are prized as food delicacies and medicines.

Unfortunately poached items can be sold at extremely high prices to collectors of animal trophies and to consumers of medicines made from animal body parts. This makes the illegal trade in endangered animals very lucrative.

AGRICULTURE To divert water to agricultural areas, some 4,290 dams have been built, 73 percent of which are in the states of Maharashtra, Madhya Pradesh, and Gujarat. Dams destroy the environment by flooding river valleys, causing silt to build up downstream and animals to move out of the area or die due to changes in marine ecology.

In a bid to increase food production, India joined the Green Revolution. Farmers were given special seeds that grew faster and produced more grain than the local varieties of food crops. But these super seeds needed chemical fertilizers, pesticides, and herbicides to grow well. These chemicals washed into the rivers, polluting the water and harming marine wildlife. The speedy growth of the special seeds also reduced soil fertility. The rice fields were flooded all year round to keep up with the increased pace of production. Thus the land had no time to lie fallow and rejuvenate after each harvest.

Women harvest crops in a rice field.

THE WORST INDUSTRIAL ACCIDENT IN HISTORY

Bhopal is a city in Madhya Pradesh whose name has become synonymous with tragedy and the dangers of the use of toxic chemicals.

On the evening of December 2, 1984, at the Union Carbide dry-cell battery manufacturing plant in Bhopal, water leaked into a storage tank containing methyl isocyanate (MIC), a very toxic chemical. Reacting with the water, the chemical vaporized and was carried in the wind to neighboring communities. The chemical's effects were immediate. Residents who did not die in bed, staggered into the streets, blinded and choked by the gas. Many were rushed to the nearest hospitals, only to die after having suffered extended pain from inhaling the gas.

Following the accident, Union Carbide closed the Bhopal plant. Five years of legal action led to the confirmation of the compensation the corporation would have to make to the Indian people for the loss and suffering caused by the accident. In 1989, the Supreme Court of India ordered Union Carbide to pay US$470 million in settlement of claims arising from the tragedy. In addition, Union Carbide later sold its interest in the Bhopal plant and contributed the proceeds to a charitable trust set up to fund the building and operation of a hospital for the victims.

Unfortunately little can be done to alleviate the environmental consequences of the 1984 accident. Toxic waste left at the Union Carbide factory has leached into the ground and polluted the wells from which the locals get drinking water. In 1999 Greenpeace reported excessive levels of a suspected carcinogen in water samples collected from the site (although tests by the Indian National Environmental Engineering Research Institute found no contamination in 100 off-site wells).

Bhopal has undoubtedly paid the world's highest price for a lesson on the environmental danger of toxic chemicals. The Madhya Pradesh state government reported that the accident resulted in approximately 3,800 deaths. Some 2,720 people suffered total or partial permanent disability, and 18,922 suffered permanent injury. The extent and severity of the Bhopal tragedy earned it a record for being the world's worst industrial accident in history.

ENVIRONMENTAL PROTECTION

CHIPKO—THE "TREE-HUGGERS" OF NORTHERN INDIA In 1973 government attempts to fell trees in the Himalayan forests to get railroad ties and pulp wood for paper production were squashed by the Chipko movement. The local people, many of whom were women and children, literally hugged the trees to stop the loggers' axes. This is how the movement got its name (*chipko* means "embrace"). This is also probably where the use of the term "tree-hugger" to refer to an environmentalist originated. The Chipko movement spread throughout the Himalayan forests, making it impossible for the government to carry out its logging plans. Finally, in 1980, Prime Minister Indira Gandhi issued an order prohibiting logging in the region for 15 years. This was a major victory for the demonstrators. The ideals and practices of the movement have since spread to the forested regions of central and south India and to the states of Himachal Pradesh, Kamataka, Rajasthan, and Bihar.

Without environmental protection, opportunities to be close to nature, such as these girls are enjoying, will grow fewer and farther between.

INDIANS

INDIA is one of the world's most ethnically diverse countries. Attempts have been made to bring ethnic groups together and create a national identity, but tensions between groups often end in violence.

It is almost impossible to categorize the Indians of today by their racial origins. It is currently accepted by historians that an early Aryan civilization—dominated by peoples whose language connected them to the people of Iran and Europe—came to occupy northwestern and then north-central India roughly between 2000 and 1500 B.C. They then moved southwest and east, imperiling the indigenous groups of those areas. Many years of invasions by other cultures followed, adding to the ethnic diversity of India.

Thus, present-day India includes a number of ethnic groups. Broadly speaking, the people in the north and northwestern regions of Kashmir, Rajasthan, Punjab, and Delhi tend to resemble European and Indo-European peoples. They are usually tall and fair, with pronounced features. The central regions of Uttar Pradesh, Madhya Pradesh, and Bihar are inhabited by people who are generally somewhat darker and shorter.

A blend of Dravidians, or indigenous Indian peoples, and Mongolians live in the eastern Indian regions of Assam, Manipur, Nagaland, and Mizoram. A Tibeto-Burman type characterized by slanting eyes and high cheekbones can be found in the Himalayan foothills.

Above: **A young Christian reading the Bible.**

Opposite: **Two Rajasthani village women.**

PEOPLE OF THE KASHMIR VALLEY

The Kashmiris and Himachalis of the north, blessed with a healthy, cold climate, are energetic, robust, and exuberant at work or leisure. Muslims, Hindus, and Buddhists live harmoniously in these Himalayan valleys.

Jammu is the land of warriors called Dogras and shepherd-nomads called Gujars. Both men and women of Kashmir wear *phiran* ("fee-rahn")—a long cloak—and *salwar* ("sehl-WAHR"), or loose pants. The women wear headdresses and large silver earrings. Muslim men wear a cap and sport a beard, while Muslim women often wear a black veil, the *burqah* ("BUR-kah"), that covers them completely.

In winter Kashmiris keep warm with a kind of portable heater. They place a *kangri* ("KAHNG-gree")—an earthen pot of burning coals—in a cane basket. They tie this round their waist and then cover themselves with a cloak or shawl that traps the heat.

Kashmiris have long-established traditions of carpet and silk weaving, lacquerware, and wooden handicrafts. They cultivate apples, corn, and legumes in terraced fields cut out of hills, and grow flowers and vegetables on floating rafts called *radhi* ("rah-di"). Some live in houseboats known as *shikaras* ("shee-KAH-rahs").

Culturally, the Himachalis have much in common with the Kashmiris. In the northern plateau of Ladakh, however, live some mountain-bound groups, mostly Tibetan Buddhists, whose isolation has helped maintain their unique customs. The people of the hilly regions in the north share a common love for folk arts and live in communion with nature, reflecting a joy in life.

Opposite top: **Punjabis are well-known for their military prowess and love of dance.**

Opposite bottom: **A brigade of Indians carrying baskets on their veiled heads.**

Below: **Ladakh spectators.**

PUNJABIS AND RAJASTHANIS

Punjab, known as the land of the five rivers and traditionally India's breadbasket, is the most fertile state. Punjabis are primarily agriculturalists who grow wheat, rice, legumes, and vegetables. Punjab is also known for its hosiery, woolens, and sports and engineering products.

Punjabis are tall and fair-skinned. The men wear loose white pants or the traditional cloth wrap—called *dhoti* ("DHOH-ti") throughout India, *tehmat* ("TEH-meht") in Punjab, and *veshti* ("VEHSH-ti"), *mundu* ("moon-do"), or *soon* ("soon") in the south—with a long shirt and a colorful turban. The women wear heavily embroidered long skirts or the Punjabi suit— loose pants and a long blouse—and usually cover their heads with a scarf or a shawl. Both men and women in the countryside love to adorn themselves with jewelry.

South of Punjab is Rajasthan, land of forts, palaces, deserts, and camels. Rajasthanis are famous for brassware, marble work, pottery, jewelry, embroidery, and painting.

Rajasthani women wear *ghagra* ("GHAH-grah"), gathered skirts that sweep the ground, and *kanchli* ("KEHNCH-lee"), or embroidered blouses. They cover their heads with brightly printed veils called *odhni* ("ODE-nee") and wear heavy jewelry.

Rajasthani men wear loose *dhoti* or *churidar* ("CHEW-ree-dahr")—tight pants—and a vest with a distinctive cut. They usually sport impressively huge moustaches and colorful turbans. Warm and good-natured, the people of Rajasthan take pride in their simplicity, honesty, and thrifty habits, the latter being almost proverbial among all Indians.

PEOPLE OF INDIA'S HEARTLAND

The largely Hindi-speaking northern and central states of Uttar Pradesh, Madhya Pradesh, and Bihar are the most densely populated regions of India. The heartland's rich mineral deposits have given rise to iron and steel industries, oil refineries, chemical plants, fertilizer factories, and paper industries, which in turn employ large numbers of people.

The rural people of India's heartland are primarily agriculturists who grow, among other crops, sugarcane, wheat, rice, and lentils. The farmers of central India rely heavily on the fertile soil of the Gangetic Plain for their livelihood. The rain-fed rivers Son, Ken, and Betwa supplement the Ganges and Yamuna rivers in watering the central farmland.

The people of the Bastar hills and the Chattisgarh plains in the central state of Madhya Pradesh hunt and work in the forests. The people of Chota Nagpur in the state of Bihar are farmers who still adhere to the archaic methods of cultivation that their ancestors practiced.

The inhabitants of India's heartland wear light clothing—generally cotton—because of the heat. Men in the rural areas wear the ubiquitous *dhoti* under a shirt, while the women wear traditional Indian clothing and decorate themselves with elaborate jewelry (as do women all over India). Jewelry is not just for decoration; it is also a form of savings that can be pawned or sold in an emergency. Only widows abstain from any form of ornamentation.

Both men and women in the cities favor Western-style attire—shirts and trousers, blouses and pants or skirts. Young children generally wear as little as possible to stay comfortable in the heat, especially when they play.

India's heartland is known also as the "pious heartland." Several religious centers such as Varanasi, Badrinath, Prayag, and Mathura—to which Indians frequently go on pilgrimage—are located in this region.

However the central Indian belt does have one notorious feature: It is plagued by professional robbers who are adept at traversing the treacherous terrain on horseback. These robbers are the bane of the state and federal authorities, not to mention their numerous victims.

Indian washermen wash and spread their laundry to dry on the banks of the Yamuna, while trishaws, bicycles, and motorcycles cross Boat Bridge.

Naga men and women—traditional hunters—wear jewelry made of bone, shell, and horn.

EASTERN INDIANS

The eastern states of Assam, Meghalaya, Nagaland, Manipur, Tripura, and Arunachal Pradesh are inhabited by several groups, including the Khasis, Garos, Jaintias, Mundas, Nagas, Ahoms, Bodos, Wanchos, and Miris. Each group has its own language, customs, and dress. The women of Mizoram and Nagaland wear a tight *sarong* ("SAH-rong") wound around them like a dress. In Assam, the women wear a *mekhela* ("meh-khay-lah"), or long skirt, and a *retir* ("reh-tir"), or blouse.

Dense hilly jungle and marshland thrive in the eastern states, where mineral deposits are abundant. Rice is the chief crop; the Assamese also grow tea. Bamboo work, cane products, and weaving are important cottage industries, and every home has a loom so the women can supplement the family income. The women of the eastern groups play a larger role than the men in both the fields and the home.

Culturally, eastern Indians have much in common with their Burmese and Nepalese neighbors.

PEOPLE OF BENGAL, SIKKIM, AND ORISSA

Calcutta, the capital city of West Bengal—vibrant with lovers of literature, music, and the arts—has its unfortunate side. It is an example of the gaping disparity between the very rich and the very poor. Calcutta's poor are homeless pavement dwellers who lead a miserable existence on the roads and bridges of the city. Poverty has driven many of them to steal and beg. Yet Calcutta is also where some of India's wealthiest Bengalis reside.

Many Bengalis in the countryside are engaged in farming and fishing. They live in huts with sloping thatch roofs. Men wear a *dhoti* and a *kurtha* ("KUR-thah"), or long shirt, while women wear a *sari*, usually white with a colored border. Bengalis love to decorate the floor at the entrance to their homes with traditional designs called *alpana* ("ehl-peh-nah").

North of West Bengal is the tiny Himalayan state of Sikkim, inhabited by Lepchas, Bhutias, and Nepalese. They wear handwoven clothes, drink yak's milk, and grow fruits, potatoes, cardamom, and barley.

Orissa, south of West Bengal, is famous for sculptured temples, dance, painting, and silver filigree. Well-endowed with rivers, it is a fertile coastal plain with large groves of coconut, mango, and palm, and fields of rice and sugarcane. Mining and jute-growing are other important occupations.

A middle-aged Bengali couple. The man wears a *dhoti* and *kurtha*.

Southern Indians gather at a communal well.

SOUTHERN INDIANS

Southern India's magnificent temples are not mere legacies of a bygone era but a living, thriving tradition. They have helped the people of the southern states to retain their heritage.

Southern Indians are the Tamils of Tamil Nadu, the Telugus of Andhra Pradesh, the Malayalees of Kerala, the Kannadigas of Karnataka, and the Tulus of the Malabar Coast.

In the countryside, Southern Indian men wear a small *dhoti* that resembles a loincloth. They are often bare-chested and barefoot. The women wear a *sari* with a short blouse. Elderly women, with earlobes stretched by heavy earrings, often wear no blouse, covering themselves deftly with just the *sari*.

The farmers of the region grow mainly rice, sugarcane, and coconuts. Some villages specialize in weaving, pottery, metal casting, or stone sculpting.

People in the southern cities reflect a mixed taste for modern and traditional values and customs, including dress; one may see women in *sari,* hair decked with flowers, going to work in a modern office. Classical music or dance lessons for every girl is the norm, while great importance is attached to education, especially in Kerala, the city with the highest literacy rate in India.

WESTERN INDIANS

Western Indians are the people of Gujarat, Goa, and Maharashtra, or Parsis who originally came from Persia, or Portuguese of mixed descent, or Caucasians who settled in western Indian ports.

Gujarati villagers grow rice, wheat, corn, sugarcane, cotton, groundnuts, and sunflower seeds. The women wear a heavily embroidered *gaghra* and a short blouse, and their heads are generally covered with an *odhni*. Gujarati men, especially from Kutch, wear tight white pants, gathered near the ankles. Their unique colorful vest is now a pan-Indian fashion.

Maharashtra's hilly Western Ghats are very fertile, being fed by a number of rivers. Rice, groundnuts, tobacco, and the famous Alphonso mangoes are grown here, in addition to cotton, the main crop. Rural Maharashtrian women tie their *sari* trouser-style, and wear large nose rings that dangle to the chin. The Goans and the women of Daman and Diu islands wear a knee-length *sari* as well as the Western-style skirt and blouse. Many men have discarded traditional clothes for shirts and trousers.

Women from a group in the Goan hills.

Mumbai, the capital city of Maharashtra, known as the Gateway of India, is the country's most important industrial city, besides being its biggest port and the nerve center of India's business and finance. Mumbai is also India's Hollywood. Residents of the city are cosmopolitan, and many adopt a Western lifestyle and outlook. The city has distinct Maharashtrian, Gujarati, Parsi, Tamil, and Sindhi areas.

LIFESTYLE

CHANGE COMES LAST AND LEAST to the countryside in traditional societies such as India. Rural life is a regular pattern of sowing, reaping, praying, and celebrating at family and social gatherings. These simple, repetitive acts have acquired a symbolic meaning over the many centuries of India's history.

The family plays a vital role. An Indian family is usually a home of three generations, rooted in a particular community. The family is also where traditional arts, handicrafts, and trades are learned and passed down. The cohesiveness of the family fosters a strong sense of belonging, and belonging is a serious and exacting concern in India. The family belongs to a particular lineage or *gotra* ("go-trah") and is identified with a particular clan or *jati* ("jah-ti") within a specific caste of a region or *kula* ("koo-lah"). Through marriage, usually planned by collective choice over individual preference, families strengthen their bonds of lineage.

Above: **Three-generation family units are the norm in India.**

Opposite: **Indian women on a joyous journey to a festival.**

Family connections are seldom lost, even when a person leaves the village for the city in pursuit of a higher education or better job prospects.

ARRANGED MARRIAGES

Arranged marriages protect family links, which are very important to people in India. Parents look for suitable life partners for their children from families of the same religion or caste. Because young Indians seldom marry outside their own religion or caste, couples can avoid problems usually caused by social or economic disparities. Through an arranged marriage, two families enter into a mutual relationship. When problems do arise in the marriage, both families try to work together to help the couple.

THE PATRIARCHAL SYSTEM

Indian society is generally patriarchal. It is usually the man who exerts ultimate authority in the family's formal relations. The father, more than the mother, has control over the children. In some instances, he makes the important family decisions for as long as he lives, even after his son has reached adulthood.

The wife and mother, however, retains dominion over informal decisions both inside and outside the home. Together, she and her husband maintain the stability of the family.

Before 1955, when the Hindu Marriage Act prohibited polygamy—marriage to more than one woman at the same time—a man could have more than one wife. In many remote villages, polygamy still exists and goes unnoticed. Polygamy is legal only among Muslims, as their religion allows it.

When it comes to having children, boys are preferred, as many Hindu rituals require a male to fulfill obligations to the ancestors. Double standards still exist for boys and girls within and outside the home. For example, parents would much rather spend on higher education for their sons than for their daughters. Also, men are favored by professional employers.

Things are changing slowly, at least in the cities, as a result of industrialization, equal education opportunities for women, and exposure to Western ideas. These trends are giving urban women greater power in the family and, gradually, in the economy.

The princely caste still commands respect. Visitors bring a *maharaja* their good wishes.

THE CASTE SYSTEM

The caste system was a social institution that divided Indian society into distinct groups. Its legacy is still apparent in many regions. In addition to the four main castes, there are hundreds of subcastes.

Although the caste system gave order to life and prescribed a code of conduct for everyone, many felt that it tended to emphasize social disparities and render the underprivileged vulnerable to exploitation. The Brahmins had access to knowledge and could thus advance to become society's elite. The Vaisya and Sudra were divided into some 3,000 subcastes, which were actually industrial guilds. The lowest social order included the garbage collectors, sweepers, and butchers—the "out-castes," the untouchables. Mahatma Gandhi called them *harijan* ("hah-ri-jahn")—children of God.

Today special attention is given to the needs of the economically backward groups, but caste consciousness is difficult to erase. In some villages, *harijan* are barred from drawing water at public wells or entering the inner sanctum of temples. Caste may be a consideration when it comes to marriage, especially in the south. Brahmins may choose to marry within their caste, as may the Chettiar moneylenders of the south and the royalty of Rajasthan. Caste identification persists. A person's neighborhood, lifestyle, food habits, speech patterns, style of dress, and family name all indicate his or her caste and lineage. However caste discrimination is waning. For example, intercaste marriages based on mutual love are on the rise, especially in the cities.

A Hindu priest reading a religious book.

More Indian women are enjoying greater freedom with access to higher education.

THE CHANGING FACES OF WOMEN

Household responsibilities are largely the woman's domain in Indian society, as is still the case in many other cultures. Also, in arranged marriages, the bride's family usually has to pay the groom's family a dowry—a gift of gold, clothes, consumer durables, or large sums of cash—that can leave a poor family debt-ridden.

But the situation is improving vastly for women in India. For example, *sati*—the medieval and scattered practice of widows burning themselves on their husband's funeral pyre—has almost disappeared, and more widows are remarrying. *Purdah* ("PERH-dah")—a system that discouraged men from addressing upper class women without a veil or screen between them—is almost nonexistent today.

Women in some Dravidian societies, especially in Kerala and Manipur, enjoy considerable freedom and equality. In Kerala, it is common for the man to marry into the woman's family, and property can pass from mother to daughter. The women of the Metei tribe in Assam also command greater socio-economic power than women elsewhere in India. There are even priestesses in the Assamese tradition.

The changing faces of women

In the fast-changing cities, the role of the working woman is a paradox. Economic independence and the popular women's liberation movement have given Indian women a new sense of freedom and confidence. But heavy demands on them at work and at home have also given rise to conflicts, increasing the rate of divorce. A number of women's periodicals discuss modern issues from fashion to premarital sex to drugs. Women vote and hold important political positions. Most urban women of means are university graduates, many of whom choose careers in medicine, academia, and law. The gender gap is narrowing, bit by bit.

Young Indian women in casual urban attire.

Schoolchildren on an excursion.

CHILDHOOD

The moment of an Indian child's birth is marked on an astrological calendar, and the child's horoscope is charted. A boy will inherit family skills and honor the household gods. A girl will in time teach her children the family traditions. The birth of a son is generally a more celebrated event, as it brings the family a potential income earner.

Indian naming ceremonies vary from region to region. Generally, on the 11th day after birth—a few days later in some communities—the child is dressed in finery and blessed with a name. The name is written on a mound of paddy (unhusked rice) or wheat, and the baby is placed on it for a while. Only then is the child believed to have overcome afterbirth complications. For Indians, human birth and plant life are analogous, and a successful birth is likened to a successful harvest.

Every milestone from then on is an occasion to celebrate, a rite to be performed, whether it is weaning from breast milk, taking the first step, ear piercing, head shaving, or the first birthday. Astrologically auspicious dates and times are selected for such events. The first step towards formal education is significant. The Hindus call this *Vidyarambha* ("vid-yah-rehm-bhah"); the Muslims, *bismillah* ("bis-mill-lah"). The Muslim priest helps the child recite a Koranic text and solemnizes formal learning.

In orthodox Hindu groups, a boy's initiation is as vital as the start of his student life. The thread ceremony, called *Upanayanam* ("oo-pah-neh-yehm"), among the warrior, priest, and merchant castes symbolizes spiritual rebirth. Amid Vedic chants, the boy undergoes rites to cleanse his body and mind. He is given three sacred threads to wear across his shoulders for the rest of his life.

A Hindu girl does not go through such formal initiation. However, in many Dravidian societies, the first time a girl menstruates is celebrated with feasting and anticipation of her marriage.

Ear piercing is common for both boys and girls. The custom began long ago, when knowledge was passed down orally. Piercing the ears was believed to sharpen children's hearing and increase their mental retention capacity.

TRADITIONAL MARRIAGE

Orthodox Hindus believe that an unmarried person has no social status. A Hindu marriage is considered a lifelong partnership, a sacred and unalterable union. Rarely is a traditional marriage entrusted to the whims of the boy or girl. The parents arrange the alliance after consulting the family elders and astrologers, matching horoscopes and comparing castes, status, and family backgrounds.

The marriage ceremony itself is rich in symbolism, and preparations usually begin weeks before the event. Ritual practice may vary in detail from region to region, but the Vedic ritual itself has remained unchanged for more than 2,000 years.

Constructing a temporary altar to the fire god Agni, the priest acts as Brahma, the creator. The bride and groom are also likened to Indian gods and goddesses: Shiva and Shakti or Vishnu and Lakshmi. The marriage is complete when the groom ties a sacred thread, called *mangala sutra* ("MEHNG-geh-lah SOO-trah"), around the bride's neck, the couple walks around the fire and recites the marriage verse from the Rig Veda, and blessings are bestowed upon them by all the elders present.

The union is thus sanctified, making divorce unthinkable in the Indian tradition. There is no equivalent for the word *divorce* in the dictionary of any of the Indian languages. *Talaq* ("tah-LAHK"), meaning divorce, is used freely in Hindi, but it is an Arabic term imported by Muslims, for whom divorce is allowed, although strongly discouraged.

An advertisement placed in a newspaper by an eligible bachelor looking for a bride. The dailies are India's modern matchmakers.

MATRIMONIAL

Alliance invited for Haritasa, Telugu Aruvela Niyogi Brahmin groom, 31. A science and law graduate currently working at Saudi and desirous of migrating to USA/Canada. As advt. is for wider choice interested parents/guardians are requested to respond soonest, along with horoscope details etc. to:

MODERN MARRIAGE

In the cities, long years of formal education have pushed the marrying age into the late 20s and the 30s. When following the traditional path of finding a partner, young urban Indians may find the classified advertisements in the newspapers' special matrimonial columns an efficient matchmaker.

The practice of paying a dowry in marriage is losing its relevance in modern life and is a legally punishable offense. Mainstream India has completely weaned off dowry marriages in favor of love marriages.

Some modern families do not mind intercaste, interregional, or even interreligious marriages, when the man and the woman have known each other for years, either at college or at the workplace. Indira Gandhi, a Hindu, married a Parsi. Some people prefer to remain single, and a handful experiment with living together without a formal commitment.

Educated Indians today have modernized the external forms of marriage. An urban Indian couple retains the basic Vedic ritual, but holds the wedding reception at a five-star hotel.

An Indian marriage ceremony.

"Take seven steps with me, my friend. Be my mate and blend with me."

—A marriage chant.

OLD AGE

Old age is a beautiful stage of life in traditional India. When a son marries and adds to the family community, his parents move up the ladder of seniority and are consulted on all important family matters. In due course, even neighbors and friends will seek their blessings on auspicious occasions.

In ancient times, when a man and his wife grew old, they were expected to give up the materialistic family life and settle in a forest, practicing a simple, spiritual way of life. Today, although the elderly do not proceed to the forest, they do make pilgrimages to religious centers and gradually relegate mundane household affairs to the younger generation. Seldom is there a clash of interests between the old and the young; where resentment exists, it is rarely revealed, out of respect for the elders.

In the cities, however, a slightly different picture emerges. Younger family members often prefer to set up their own homes, either to be closer to their workplace or because the joint family structure no longer appeals to them. Families meet only during festivals and family celebrations. Retirees feel less inclined to rely on their children, and a growing number save up for their future. But although they are more self-reliant financially, the aged in the cities are less prepared emotionally. They face very real problems of loneliness, due to the breakdown of the extended family.

THE HINDU VIEW OF LIFE AND DEATH

Since reincarnation is a basic tenet of Hinduism, to the Hindu, life is a ceaseless cycle of events that begins where it ends. Death is merely a stage in that cycle, as inevitable as birth itself. Therefore, death is not final, just a transfer of the soul from one body to another, quite like casting off old clothes to wear new ones.

Whether one is reborn as a plant, insect, animal, or human being, and whether one's new life is a happy and prosperous one or filled with trials and tribulations depends on one's previous life. Hindus believe that a truly noble life, with good thoughts, words, and deeds, will release the soul from the life and death cycles and secure eternal liberation, called *moksha* ("mohk-shah"). The Buddhists call this *nirvana* ("nir-VAH-nah")—attaining a state of nothingness.

While Hindus perform several rites during their lifetime, surviving relatives perform last rites for a person's well-being in the next life. Failure to perform these rites would cause their soul to wander without a place in the next world. Only a son can perform the last rites for his father, which explains some of the traditional bias for sons.

The eldest son usually performs the last rites with the help of a priest. The dead body is dressed in new clothes, placed on a bier, and taken to the cremation grounds, amid the chanting of God's name. The pyre is lit, the body cremated, and the ashes collected the next day for immersion in the holy Ganges River. Thirteen days of mourning begin, to be completed with a ritual and a feast, both of which suggest a return to normality.

Although cremation is the norm among Hindus, young children and persons held in very great reverence are buried; so are Muslims and Christians. Victims of epidemics are generally cast away in water so as not to offend the evil spirits that have attacked the victim.

"Life is a stage with one entrance and many exits."

—*A Hindu saying.*

KARMA

Karma ("kahr-mah") is a fundamental belief among Indians, especially Hindus and Buddhists, that means "action." Like the principle of cause and effect, good turns fetch a reward of good life, while bad words and deeds affect not just this life but the next as well. Logically, therefore, a person's birth in this life is determined by the cumulative good or bad actions of his or her previous lives.

Karma offers explanations for the inequalities of life—such as why one person may be born poor or handicapped or may suffer a series of hardships, while another, even if born to the same family, enjoys peace and prosperity. *Karma* blames humans themselves, not God, for their state of poverty or ignorance.

Belief in *karma* has generally made Indians passively accept their state of poverty. Although belief in *karma* does not mean a fatalistic pessimism, the man in the countryside will always talk of his karma, whether his crops fail or his son fails! It allows him to face without flinching those hardships he cannot avert.

Indians also believe that stars and planets affect the individual, and that the elements of earth, water, fire, wind, and space rule man's health and well-being. Many of their beliefs have foundation in the ancient sciences of astrology and medicine. In Indian society, where faith involves belief in the supernatural and myths are still alive, faith often gets mixed with strange superstitions.

SUPERSTITIONS

If superstitions are caused by humans' fear of the unknown, it is clear why they are an integral part of any traditional society. Indians may use the

Gregorian calendar for their daily transactions, but when it comes to buying property, starting a business venture, or even moving, they go by the Indian astrological calendar. In this, even numbers are regarded as auspicious. Generally, eight and nine are good, while seven is not. Wednesday is good for traveling and Friday for sacred matters. On Friday, meat is taboo, a visit to the barber frowned upon, and visiting the home of a bereaved person simply out of the question.

A fortuneteller with a client. Astrologers and fortunetellers are part of the fabric of Indian society.

Some of these things may be customs and beliefs, but the label *superstition* takes over when meaning is attached to events beyond human control. For instance, if someone sneezes before a project starts, it will not be completed; if a lizard falls on one's head, death is imminent; if a dog howls, it is the call of Yama, the god of death. The list is endless.

No one knows how some of these superstitions came about, but the *Puranas* tell frightening tales of what befalls those who do not believe in ancient practices.

These old stories also prescribe antidotes. Thus, practices such as bathing in the holy Ganges River to wash away one's sins, or offering one's hair to the Lord as a symbol of sacrifice may appear superstitious to some but are religious obligations for the millions living in India.

RITUALS AND SACRIFICES

Quite apart from the city dwellers or the villagers, live small groups with unique customs that reveal an intimate relationship with the spirits. Whether it is to seek a good harvest or to cure an illness, the entire community is pressed into service for ancient magical rituals.

Using mystical and sometimes occult powers, they rely upon sorcery and witchcraft to purify wayward souls and victims of the evil eye. The entire community is quarantined, if untimely deaths or epidemics occur. Along with strict taboos, which are observed for a period of several days, rituals are performed by witch doctors to appease high-ranking spirits and return the evil to its initiators.

Spirits are believed to reside in trees, plants, hills, springs, iron implements, diseases like chicken pox—anything the group fears or reveres. Specialist mediums are believed to remove the curse of evil by communicating with the spirits through trances and divination.

Sacrifices may be offered. To satisfy the earth's demands, the Konds of central India make ritual sacrifices to the earth goddess. Strips of animal flesh are buried in the soil to ensure fertility.

These disparate groups are slowly being modernized by education and social interaction, though many still hold on to their inclination for isolation.

Opposite top: **Water pots have to be filled at the communal well.**

Opposite bottom: **Village women weave cloth for their own use as well as to supplement the family income.**

Below: **A ritual dance before the hunt.**

VILLAGE LIFE

Except for a few regional differences, village life is basically the same all over India. Villagers wake up at dawn and take a quick bath in a nearby pond, river, or well. They chew twigs of the neem tree or rub tooth powder with their right index finger to clean their teeth. On special days, villagers especially in the south massage oil over their bodies and rinse with indigenous herbs and powders. The laundry is done by beating the clothes on rough stones and scrubbing them with soap.

Coffee is the beverage of the south, while tea is standard in the north. Seated on the floor, Indians eat either food left over from the previous night's meal or porridge made from rice, millet, or wheat. Then the men proceed to the fields or workplace, the children to schools, and the women to fetch water or firewood.

Everyone returns before sunset to tend to the cows and goats in their sheds, play traditional games, watch village shows, or attend temple festivals. There is plenty of leisure time for entertainment and social interaction. Evenings are for gossiping about politics or village affairs. Then, after checking that the animals have been fed and the water pots filled for the next day's chores, the villagers go to sleep on mats spread out on the floor.

CITY LIFE

City life in India presents many sharp contrasts. Apart from the wealth and poverty revealed by the coexistence and juxtaposition of slums and luxurious mansions, the city centers are generally congested.

High demand and short supply have created shortages of housing, water, electricity, telephone service, transportation facilities, places in schools and universities, and employment opportunities. More and more Indians now seek employment abroad, especially in the newly industrialized countries of Southeast Asia, such as Malaysia and Singapore. More money to spend has led to growing consumerism.

Yet life in Indian cities can be rewarding. The people are caring and warm. Whether it is reaching out to a neighbor or extending hospitality to a stranger, Indians respond readily, almost instinctively.

Urban dwellers are increasingly becoming lovers of classical Indian art, making the cities vibrant with music and dance festivals that last several weeks in some seasons. The growth of art institutions reflects a growing interest in art among Indian youths. It has even become fashionable to use ethnic textiles and folk handicrafts. India's age-old traditions look set to live on into the information age.

Above: **Getting on the bus—literally. This is child's play to seasoned bus riders.**

Opposite: **Bicycles and scooters are common modes of transportation. Cars, trucks, rickshaws, and bullock carts often come together on narrow streets, increasing travel time and the risk of accidents.**

RELIGION

INDIA IS A SECULAR COUNTRY. The assimilation of various religious values has generally created tolerance among the different groups. However, religious unrest does occur and has been a problem when politicians have exploited the people's religious differences. Most clashes occur between Hindus and Muslims, the largest religious minority in India. One such incident took place in December 1992, when Hindus tore down the 16th-century Babri mosque in Ayodhya, claiming that it had been built over the birthplace of Rama.

The world's major religions have found a home in India, where Hinduism and Buddhism were born. Nearly 80 percent of the population is Hindu, with the rest professing Islam, Christianity, Sikhism, Buddhism, Jainism, Judaism, or Zoroastrianism.

Religion plays an important part in Indian life. Joyous occasions are celebrated with a visit to a mosque, temple, or shrine, and it is common for Indians to make religious processions and pilgrimages, regardless of

what faith they profess. Virtually every day of the year marks a festive occasion in the calendar of one faith or another.

Indians display symbols of their faith at the front door of their home to invoke blessings from the gods and heavenly protection over the household. Christians adorn their doors with the cross, Muslims with a verse from the Koran, and Hindus with a picture of Ganesha, the god who wards off evil.

Opposite: **The Bahai temple in India. Bahai has Persian roots. Freedom to practice any religion is a fundamental right in India.**

Left: **Prayer at dawn on the ghats by the Ganges River in Varanasi.**

73

HINDUISM

Hinduism is one of the oldest living faiths in the world and forms the ethos of the majority of Indians. It is important to understand this faith in order to understand the people who practice it, particularly since Hinduism is more a way of life than a religion.

Unlike many other faiths, Hinduism does not have a founder. Nor is it based on any single scripture. Indians call it *Sanatama Dharma*—the faith with no beginning and no end.

Hinduism offers different approaches to persons of different aptitudes. It does not prescribe rules. Rather, it reveals profound truths about life and suggests various paths of righteous living. As the choice of a path is left to the believer, the religion means different things to different people. One can understand aspects of the religion by examining its essential features, starting with the Vedas. These are sacred texts containing hymns of creation, prayers, and philosophical discussions.

To simplify high philosophy and offer it to the common people, legends were created. The *Puranas*, the *Ramayana*, and the *Mahabharata* are stories that drive home universal values of righteous living.

A part of the Mahabharata is the *Bhagavad Gita*, a philosophical song of God that brings out the essence of Hinduism in simple form. Here, Lord Krishna advocates three paths: the path of mental discipline for the intellectual; the pursuit of love and devotion for the emotional; and the path of selfless service for those who believe that "work is worship." And for all, Lord Krishna advocates nonviolence, truth, and detachment.

Opposite bottom: **A Hindu priest blesses devotees.**

Below: **A monumental and intricately carved** *gopuram* **or gateway to a Hindu temple.**

HINDU VALUES Hinduism does not deny one the enjoyment of life. It advocates the pursuit of four goals: *dharma* ("dhahr-mah"), *artha* ("ahr-thah"), *kama* ("kah-mah"), and *moksha* ("mock-shah"). These translate roughly as righteous living, wealth and prosperity, love and happiness, and release from the cycle of births and deaths.

Hindus strive to pursue the right action at the right time. Life is roughly divided into four stages: childhood, a time of joy and innocence; student life, a time of discipline in mind and body; married life, a time for family and the household; and old age, a time to renounce material things in preparation for the final years. Since these stages are common to everyone, Hindu priests can also marry and raise families.

Hindu gods and goddesses reflect the Hindu value system. Anything beautiful, valuable, or awe-inspiring is associated with divinity. Plant and animal life, natural forces of energy, the sun, the planets, the elements, art, knowledge, wealth, and happiness all have their corresponding deities.

Amid this host of gods and goddesses is the concept of the Hindu Trinity: Brahma the Creator, Vishnu the Preserver, and Shiva the Destroyer. Together, they symbolize the ultimate god known as Brahman, represented by the formless sound symbol, *Aum* ("ohm"). (Brahman should not be confused with the priestly caste known as Brahmin.)

Although Hindus believe that all these gods are different manifestations of one supreme God, the deities are very real to them. The gods' birthdays and marriage anniversaries are occasions for celebration in homes and temples. Hinduism really comes alive during such festivals.

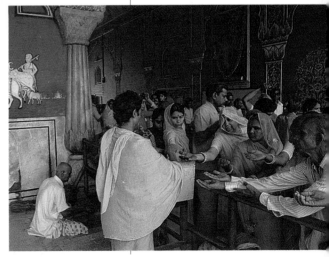

Right: **Morning prayers.**

*Opposite: **Linga Puja**—a prayer to Shiva in the shape of a black mound, over which is the sacred pot containing milk, the life-sustaining fluid.*

HINDU RITUALS AND BELIEFS Rituals are part of the Hindu way of life. From birth to death, Hindus must observe various ceremonies in order to achieve total development. Although some of these rituals and customs are now obsolete, many are followed to this day. These rituals are imbued with rich symbolism. Each is a prayer for prosperity and offspring in this life and the next.

The cow is sacred to Hindus. They worship it as the Divine Mother, so eating beef is taboo. (This taboo was one of the sparks of the Sepoy Revolt of 1857; see page 24.) The cow is the source of life-sustaining milk and also the symbol of fertility. Every animal, in fact, is associated with a god: the elephant with Ganesha, the snake with Vishnu, the bull with Shiva, the peacock with Mùrugan, the swan with Brahma, and so on. This association of gods with animals is one of the reasons why many Hindus are vegetarians. Some Hindus refrain from meat by choice, others because of caste considerations.

Water is sacred to Hindus. Many pious Hindus feel blessed after a dip in the river, in particular the Ganges. Most temples have a pond in the courtyard for bathing.

IMAGES OF LIFE

During the Ganapati festival in western India and Durga Puja in Bengal, huge images of deities are installed and consecrated. This is known as the life-giving ceremony. After 10 days of prayers and offerings, the images are taken on a procession and ceremonially immersed in a river, pond, or sea, suggesting a renewal and rebirth for the gods.

BUDDHISM

Buddhism was founded in the sixth century B.C. and spread across the whole of Asia. But it was eclipsed as a distinct religion in India some time around the 12th century A.D. Many Buddhist ways were absorbed into Hinduism, and Buddha became one of the incarnations of the Hindu god, Vishnu.

The early 20th century saw a Buddhist revival movement led by Dr. B.R. Ambedkar, as a result of which there are more than four million Buddhists in India today. The majority live in the state of Maharashtra. The Himalayan regions of Ladakh and Leh, however, have remained Buddhist since ancient times.

Buddhism stands on three pillars: Buddha, its founder; Dharma, his teachings; and Sangha, the order of monkhood. The essence of Buddhism lies in the Four Noble Truths and the Eightfold Path. Buddha taught that desire is the root of all suffering and that detachment and freedom from desire can lead to higher wisdom. The Eightfold Path is in correct understanding, thought, speech, action, livelihood, effort, mind, and meditation. Following this path, Buddhists can free themselves of ignorance, control their senses, and attain *nirvana*, or release from the cycle of births and deaths.

Buddhism was divided into three schools a few centuries after Buddha's death. Theravada, the original form, is practiced in India, Burma, Sri Lanka, and Thailand. The easier-to-follow teachings of the Mahayana sect are popular in Tibet, China, Korea, and Japan. Vajrayana is an esoteric offshoot of Mahayana that introduced magic, mysticism, and the worship of male-female union. Japanese Zen is the meditative aspect of Buddhism known as Dhyana.

Two Buddhist novices rest in a shelter.

JAINISM

Jina, meaning "one who has conquered the senses," is the name given to Vardhamana Mahavira, the great reformer and religious leader who lived in Buddha's time. Mahavira's followers, known as Jains, practice control of the senses. Although Jainism developed before Buddhism and spread through southern India, it has only about three million followers, mainly among the merchant communities of Gujarat, Uttar Pradesh, and Rajasthan.

In the past, Jains contributed substantially to India's social and cultural life. Many Hindu practices, such as vegetarianism and fasting, are of Jain origin. Jains adhere to a strict physical and mental discipline. Through a rigorous code of morality, self-denial, and nonviolence, they strive to achieve salvation. To this day, orthodox Jains abstain from onions and garlic—said to increase sensual desires—and fermented edibles for fear of harming living bacteria.

Jains and Hindus have merged in several ways: in intermarriage and certain festivals and in the worship of Lakshmi, the goddess of wealth. The Jain symbol is the swastika, auspicious to Hindus and Buddhists.

There are two main sects of Jainism. The Swetambaras worship a Mahavira dressed in a white robe. The Digambaras worship an unadorned Mahavira, a huge statue of whom stands majestically at Sravanabelagola in Mysore.

A Jain ceremony.

The Golden Temple in Amritsar, with a good view of the *sarovar* ("sah-roh-vahr"), or holy water tank, around it.

SIKHISM

The word *Sikh* is derived from the Sanskrit *shiksh*, which means "to learn." In the Punjabi language, it refers to a learner or a disciple. The followers of Guru Nanak and his nine spiritual successors have come to be known as Sikhs. Guru Nanak's sayings and verses are found in the holy book of *Guru Granth Sahib*, which Sikhs venerate in their homes and in *gurdwaras* ("gurd-wah-rahs"), or temples.

Guru Nanak, the founding teacher of Sikhism, was born in 1469 in a village called Talwandi Rai Bhoe, now in Pakistan. Guru Nanak was spiritual even as a young boy, rejecting caste and religious distinctions and preaching the doctrine of One God, which he simply called *Ikk* ("ache"), One. He felt that God could be perceived through loving devotion.

Sikhism grew into an institution only under the fifth teacher, Guru Arjan, in the 16th century. He constructed the Harimandir, the Golden Temple at Amritsar, the holiest Sikh shrine today. His successor, Guru Hargobind, adorned himself with two swords and gave a martial direction to Sikhism. Within a century from then, Sikhism became a cohesive social and political force.

Traditional Sikh men are easily identified by a beard, a steel bangle, and a turban covering hair uncut since birth. They also carry a small knife symbolizing their readiness to defend their faith and fight injustice. However, many modern Sikh men no longer follow these customs.

Sikhs are believed to make good warriors due to a fearless tenacity, indicated by their surname, Singh, which means "lion." Culturally, Sikhs are like the Hindus of the Punjab region, and intermarriage used to be common. Since 1980, however, tension and violence between Sikhs and Hindus have been increasing, with an extremist group calling for an independent Sikh homeland, Khalistan, meaning Land of the Pure.

Sikh devotees inside the Golden Temple.

ISLAM

Islam was imported into India by Muslim conquerors and Arab merchants in the 10th century A.D. Many Hindus were forced to convert. Some were offered economic incentives as a reward, while others were drawn by Islam's high ideal of universal brotherhood.

Islam is an Arabic word meaning "submission to God" and "peace." Its founder, Prophet Mohammed, was born in Mecca in the sixth century A.D. Muslims believe that he received divine messages from God and that these messages are collected in the sacred book, the Koran.

All Muslims follow certain basic principles enshrined in the Koran. They must profess their faith in Allah, the one ultimate God, recite prayers five times a day, fast during the month of Ramadan, give a part of their wealth to charity, and go on a Haj (pilgrimage to Mecca) at least once in their lifetime if they can afford it.

Islam spread throughout India, but the Muslim population today is concentrated in the states of Uttar Pradesh, Bengal, Kashmir, Kerala, Hyderabad, Tamil Nadu, and Gujarat. Indian Muslims work in many sectors of the economy, but most are merchants, artists, and artisans. There are two main Islamic sects: Shia and Sunni. Indian Muslims are mostly Sunni. Some practice Sufism, a mystical doctrine that emphasizes direct communion with God through intuitive knowledge.

CHRISTIANITY

India's Christians belong to several groups and churches. About four million Indians belong to the Church of St. Thomas. These are known as Syrian Christians. St. Thomas is believed to have arrived in Cochin to spread the message of Jesus Christ in the first century A.D. The arrival of the Portuguese in Goa and the French in Pondicherry in the Middle Ages brought fresh infusions of Catholicism to these parts.

The 18th and 19th centuries, when the British entrenched themselves in India, saw the spread of English Protestantism, mainly in eastern India, through educational and charitable institutions. Marriages between Indians and Europeans also resulted in an ethnic subgroup of Christian Anglo-Indians in this area.

Today there are some 25 million Christians contributing to all sectors of Indian society. While many Christians in the larger cities, such as Mumbai and Calcutta, have adopted Western values and customs, the Christians of southern India, particularly in the suburbs and villages, can hardly be distinguished from their Hindu neighbors, with whom they share many customs and beliefs.

SAINT OF THE GUTTER

Mother Teresa (*right*) was born in 1910 in Skopje, Yugoslavia. In 1950 she founded an order of nuns, called the Missionaries of Charity, in Calcutta. She gave the rest of her life to the care of the poorest of the poor in India and became known as the "Saint of the Gutter." Starting with 12 sisters in India, the Missionaries of Charity have grown to more than 3,000 in 517 missions in 100 countries.

Mother Teresa won the Nobel Peace Prize in 1979. She died in 1997.

ZOROASTRIANISM

Zoroastrianism takes its name from its founder, Zoroaster, a Persian prophet who pondered life and existence and realized that absolute energy lies in perfect wisdom, which he called Ahura Mazda. His followers are known as Zoroastrians or Parsis. Zoroastrianism is the oldest living religion.

Preceding all other philosophies in India, Zoroastrianism influenced the Indo-Aryan Vedic philosophy in the early periods, although it was only in the eighth century A.D. that a group of Persian Zoroastrians, persecuted by Muslims in their own land, set sail towards Kathiawar and Sanjan in western India and settled there.

Gradually, they spread in small colonies, retaining their religious identity but adopting local customs. Known as Parsis (people of Persia), they make up an extremely tiny percentage of the Indian population. They were originally farmers, weavers, and toddy-palm planters, but today they are some of India's biggest industrialists.

The holy book of Zendavestha contains the founder's sayings, known as *gathas* ("gah-thahs"). It advocates the worship of Ahu, the source and moving force of life. The luminous sun and the radiant fire are Zoroastrian symbols. The Parsis worship fire in their temples and always have a lighted lamp in their homes.

Parsi moral values stem from the motto, "Good thoughts, good speech, and good deeds lead to perfect wisdom." The ceremonies exclusive to Parsis are Navjoth, the initiation into Zoroastrian ways, and *ateti* ("ah-tay-ti") or Navroze, the Parsi New Year. A distinctive feature is the Parsi funeral ceremony, when after prayers the body is offered to vultures and other birds of prey on top of a high hill, the Tower of Silence. The bones are then lowered into wells for dissolution.

TANTRIKAS

Tantrika is a spiritual tradition often associated with spells and dark deeds, though this is not a completely accurate view.

Early Tantrika followers questioned the supremacy of the *Vedas*, rejected the Hindu caste system, and dismissed the possibility of life after death. Their desire for prosperity "here and now" brought fertility cults of the mother-goddess into the Tantrik fold. With this came the secret art of worshiping the life-giving sexual principle. In the Western world today, Tantrika is often strongly associated with sex.

Using elaborate diagrams, chants, charms, and hand gestures, the rituals of the Tantrikas are an attempt to "bring to life" objects of worship. Tantrika followers practice yoga, a form of exercise that unites the body with the mind. They look upon the creation of the universe as the blissful union of heaven and earth, spirit and form, and masculine and feminine principles.

Perched on top of a huge rock, a yogi meditates.

While much of Tantrik philosophy has been absorbed into the Hindu religion, some other Tantrik practices have been rejected by most Hindus and Tantrikas. These activities—black magic performances and the casting of spells to gain control over people—are carried out by obscure groups that often operate in secrecy, headed by leaders who shun public scrutiny.

LANGUAGE

A WESTERN SCHOLAR ONCE OBSERVED, "Every Indian district has its own language and customs." There are more than 400 districts in India, and numerous dialects are spoken in these districts. India's 25 states have been formed not by geopolitical divisions, but rather on the basis of the dominant language spoken in an area.

The Indian Constitution recognizes 15 state languages. Hindi and English are the country's official languages. The education system includes the study of three languages in school: Hindi, English, and the vernacular state language. This helps in developing multilingualism, while promoting the two official languages.

From ancient times until about the 11th century A.D., there were two dominant language groups in India: the Prakrit languages in the north and the Tamil languages in the south. Pali, adopted by the early Buddhists, was an offshoot of Prakrit, while Sanskrit served as the classical literary language of India, much as Latin did in the West. The development of India's languages, each with its own distinct script and literature, was a phenomenon of the medieval period. Sanskrit was increasingly absorbed into the existing vernacular dialects, and philosophical and religious texts were mass-produced in many languages. Thus the vernacular dialects gradually assumed distinct literary styles.

Today the two most widely used language groups are the Indo-Aryan and the Dravidian groups. Sanskrit belongs to the Indo-Aryan group. The ideas conveyed in texts of different languages, however, were commonly drawn from Sanskrit, which is considered the ancestor of most Indian languages. Thus, though Indian languages may appear to be quite different, they do reflect a common culture.

Hindi and its variants are spoken by more than 40 percent and understood by more than 75 percent of the population.

Opposite: **Indian calligraphy, a fine art form, carved on a wall.**

SCRIPTS

Indian scripts also have a common source. The earliest script, used until the sixth century A.D., for both Tamil and Sanskrit, was Brahmi.

Writing was not, however, the mode of transmitting knowledge in ancient India. Sitting close to the *guru* ("goo-roo"), or teacher, the pupil learned verses orally through recitation. Yet, as early as the fourth century B.C., India had not only a well-developed script, but also the greatest of all known grammarians, Panini.

Today, all 15 recognized state languages have their own scripts, derived mainly from the Indo-Aryan Sanskrit and the Dravidian Tamil. They are Assamese, Bengali, Gujarati, Hindi, Kannada, Kashmiri, Malayalam, Marathi, Oriya, Punjabi, Sanskrit, Sindhi, Tamil, Telugu, and Urdu. Urdu, a product of Indo-Muslim fusion, is generally used by the Muslim community.

English, introduced in education in the 19th century, has become a linguistic link for Indians throughout the subcontinent. The language is also an important factor in modernization, though its use is limited to the towns and cities.

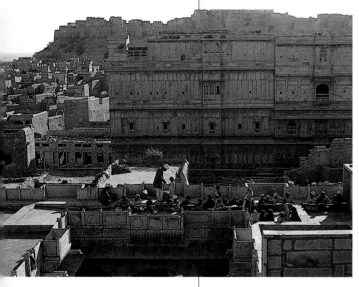

A rooftop classroom in a Rajasthan fort.

HOLY CORDS

Palm leaves and tree bark once served as writing material, and an iron stylus served as a pen. The stylus inscribed the letters on the leaves, which were smeared with ink to darken the inscription. Excess ink on the leaf surface was wiped away. The bark and leaves were strung together on a cord, so that all holy texts came to be called *sutras* ("soo-trahs"), or cords.

TAMIL TRADITION

The only writings that predate the influence of classical Sanskrit are in Tamil. Tamil literature seems to have begun with anthologies of secular lyrics, known as *sangam* ("sehng-gehm") poetry. Considered the literary masterpieces of pre-Christian times, they contain some 1,600 verses. Unlike *sangam* poetry (and, incidentally, modern Tamil literature), most traditional Tamil literature is religious in form and content.

In the very early Christian era, a sage named Tiruvalluvar (first or second century A.D.), possibly a Jain monk, wrote beautifully precise moral aphorisms that are still taught to children. The fourth to ninth centuries A.D. saw the growth of intensely rich devotional Tamil poems, forerunners to medieval Indian literature. They were songs in praise of the legendary

Children learning the alphabet in a village classroom.

gods, Shiva, Vishnu, and Krishna. The poet-saints who wrote them were called Alwars and Nayanmars.

Two romantic epics, *Silappadigaram* and *Manimekhalai*, were also composed between the second and fifth centuries A.D. The Tamil version of the Hindu epic *Ramayana* was composed with great eloquence by Kamban, a 10th-century poet.

Tamil literature thereafter went into a deep slumber, perhaps because of political changes. Among modern poets, Arunachala Kavi and Subramanya Bharatiyar stand out for their simple and narrative forms of poetry. Mahakkavi Subramanya Bharathiyar is regarded as one of the greatest Tamil poets of the 20th century.

SOUTHERN LANGUAGES

The regional languages of southern India include four of India's official languages: Telugu, the state language of Andhra Pradesh; Tamil, the state language of Tamil Nadu; Kannada, the state language of Karnataka; and Malayalam, the state language of Kerala. The southern languages contain many words from Sanskrit, the court language of many rulers in southern India between the eighth and 15th centuries and have a recorded history of more than 2,000 years.

The greatest Telugu poetry was produced during the time of the Vijayanagara Empire in the 16th century. The king, Krishna Deva Raja, was himself a renowned poet. The 16th and 17th centuries were a golden period for Telugu literature, especially in southern India. Telugu became the language of the south, after Saint Thyagaraja began singing the *raga* ("rah-gah"), emotionally charged lyrical verses in classical melodies.

Kannada also produced devotional poetry, the greatest of which was the 10,000-verse ballad, *Bharatesha Vaibhava,* written by the 16th-century poet, Ratnakarvarni Varni. Inscriptions in Kannada dating from the sixth century A.D. have been found. Among the earliest literary works are the *Kavirajamarga,* written around 850, and *Lilavati,* a royal love story written in 1370. One of the most famous works is the *Rajasekharavilasa,* a morality tale written in 1657 about Shiva's rescue of a royal family from tragedy.

A dialect that has adopted the Kannada script is Tulu, widely spoken in the Malabar region.

Malayalam seems to have existed even earlier than the ninth century. Some of the literature produced in Malayalam suggests a strong Buddhist influence. Apart from mystical verses or *champus* ("chahm-poos"), Malayalam developed a variety of dramatic literature suited for dance dramas known as Kathakali.

NORTHERN LANGUAGES

Although Prakrit is recognized as the forerunner to the northern Indian languages, it would not be easy for someone who knows one of these languages to understand another without adequate exposure. Every language has produced its own literary masterpieces, some of which have crossed linguistic divisions and become famous throughout India.

Greatest among the vernacular literati was the 20th-century poet, dramatist, and artist, Rabindranath Tagore (1861–1941) of Bengal, who won the Nobel prize for his poetry. He evokes a unique sense of reverence among Indians in general and the Bengalis in particular.

Rabindranath Tagore.

SANSKRIT LITERATURE

The earliest Sanskrit literature, the Vedas, probably dates back to 1500 B.C. Since the hymns were passed down orally for several centuries before being written down, nobody knows their exact origin. The first text, the Rig Veda, consists of 1,028 hymns in praise of the gods of nature; the Sama Veda is composed as musical mantras; the Yajureda is a book of mystical formulas; and the Atharva Veda contains magic and charms as medical prescriptions. Believed to be divinely inspired, these four Vedas became the repository of all knowledge in India. As Vedic philosophy was difficult to understand, old world legends known as Puranas were born. These imaginative tales about gods and goddesses helped the common people understand ethical values. Sanskrit dominated the literary scene for over a thousand years, inspiring the growth of several languages in India and parts of Asia and living up to its epithet, language of the gods.

Saint Kabir

A Hindu devotee reading the *Ramayana*.

HINDI

Hindi is a product of several dialects spoken in central and northern India. All of them are folk dialects that trace their roots to Prakrit. Pure Hindi uses a liberal dose of Sanskrit and many Urdu words. Indians regard Hindi as ideal for communication but readily switch to English when it comes to technical subjects.

Several Hindu and Sufi mystics contributed to the enrichment of Hindi in the medieval period. The most outstanding was the 15th-century poet, Saint Kabir. His soul-stirring verses, containing a fusion of Hindu and Muslim beliefs, are a landmark in the growth of Hindi.

The greatest Hindi poet to date, however, is the 16th-century saint, Goswami Tulsidas, whose devotional epic, *Ram Charith Manas*, retold the *Ramayana* in the language of the masses, making the scripture accessible to the layperson.

Modern Hindi prose began only in the 20th century, with writers like Mahavir Prasad Dwivedi and Mythili Sharan Gupta.

An offshoot of Hindi is Urdu (a word that means "military camp" in Turkish). Urdu began as a campsite language of Hindu and Muslim soldiers in the Hyderabad region of southern India and then acquired Hindi vocabulary and Arabic script, thus blending languages, thoughts, and beliefs.

Prolific Urdu poets appreciated both in India and Pakistan include Ghalib; the 20th-century poet Mohammed Iqbal; and Bahadur Shah Zafar, the last of the Mughal emperors.

GESTURES AND EXPRESSIONS

India's oral tradition has many gestures, expressions, and proverbs. Greetings among friends invariably invoke a god's name. *Jai Ramji ki* ("jye rahm-jee kee"), meaning "May Lord Rama be victorious and protect us," is a common greeting in the rural areas in the north, while *vanakkam swami* ("veh-neh-kehm swah-mi"), meaning "I bow to you, divine one," is a welcome in the south.

It is considered respectful to touch the feet of elders or prostrate oneself before them. The expression when leaving is "I'll go and come back" or "I'll be back," never simply "I'm going." In any Indian dialect, the latter suggests one is leaving this life.

It is common to address any man, friend or stranger, as *bhai* ("bhye"), or brother, and any woman as *behen* ("beh-hane"), or sister. The correct form of address during speeches is *bhaiyo or beheno* ("bhye-yoh or beh-hane-noh"), meaning "brothers and sisters."

An amazing uniformity exists in the oral tradition. Proverbs, such as "one who cannot dance blames the stage or finds fault with the floor" and "a dog's tail can never be straightened," are used in every dialect.

English has greatly influenced language and literature over the last 200 years. Prose literature and blank verse have invaded the literary world. It is now common in India to think in English and speak in the mother tongue or vice versa.

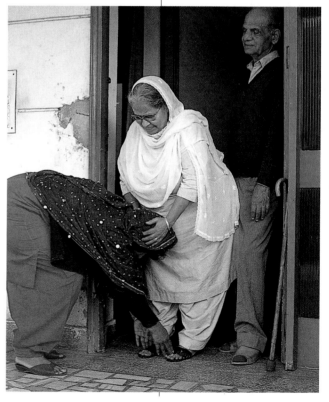

A woman touches the feet of an elder in greeting.

ARTS

ART IS A PREOCCUPATION IN INDIA, more an expression of a way of life than a pastime. It reflects India's philosophy, and its origins are as old as the history of the subcontinent. It has grown and developed at different levels to serve different functions. Whether it is jewelry beaten out of metal, delicate woven shawls and brocade *saris*, or carved wood and stone, few other nations have so exuberant a variety of arts.

The Indian performing arts do not have well-defined categories, such as the Western forms of opera, ballet, dance, or drama. Very often they are an interesting blend of all these forms. Folk, ritual, and classical elements exist side by side, influencing one another.

Yet broad classifications of the Indian arts are possible according to region, style, and purpose. The folk arts, for instance, may be connected with social revelry to celebrate successful hunting, fishing, or harvesting. The ritual or ceremonial arts are generally of the mystical variety, performed in temples as fertility rites. The classical arts of dance and music are highly stylized and refined and require years of training and academic scholarship.

Whatever the style or form, Indian arts convey a single theme: *rasa* ("rah-sah"), the essence of the joy of life. All Indian arts fuse with religious devotion, and this applies equally to music, dance, drama, poetry, painting, sculpture, and handicrafts.

Below: **The sure and deft strokes required for hand-painting take a great deal of practice.**

Opposite: **A trained dancer expresses herself in her motions and dress.**

Northern Indian villagers celebrate the Basant Panchami—one of the many Indian spring festivals—with a dance.

FOLK ART

Whether it is to celebrate spring or the monsoon season, the birthday of a mythic god, or the installation of a deity, festival time in rural India means adorning the village cows, elephants, and camels and decorating streets and homes with folk motifs symbolizing prosperity and abundance. The nights are filled with singing and dancing, and tales of gods and goddesses are played out.

Each region has its own style and form of dance. Punjab is famous for its rugged Bhangra, while Gujarat is known for its gentler Garba and Raas dances. The southern Indian street dances are called Therukkuthu, while Kavadi and Karagam are more ritualistic dances performed by devotees as wish-fulfilling prayers.

Community dances—such as the Lama dances of the Himalayan region and the Chou dance of eastern India—may involve magic, sorcery, or religious ritual. The Theyiattam dance of Kerala incorporates drama into rhythm and movement for fuller expression. To the music of powerful percussion instruments, the dancers recreate awesome characters in myths depicting the victory of good over evil.

POETRY

All classical Indian art forms can be traced back to poetry. The recitation of the Vedas is believed to have given rise to musical notes and scales. To this day it is poetry that is rendered as classical music. Classical dance too captures the poet's innermost feelings through mime and hand gestures. Dance is thought of as visual poetry, sculpture as frozen poetry.

In fact, most ancient works—fables, epic tales, and mathematical, scientific, and philosophical works—were composed in poetic form. Verse, with the rhyme and regular meter, was easier to memorize and transmit orally. Prose is a comparatively recent phenomenon.

Apart from the abundant religious literature in India—especially the *Mahabharata* and the *Ramayana*—Kalidasa's *Shakkuntalam* in Sanskrit and Ilango Adigal's *Silappadigaram* in Tamil are among the famous secular works of ancient India. In modern times, Ayyappa Paniker's *Kurukshetram* is considered a Malayalam masterpiece and has been translated into other languages, including Hindi, French, and English.

The 1930s nurtured a new generation of poets. The progressive poets drew inspiration from Marx and focused on the themes of political and social revolution in their poems. They concentrated on ideas and ideology rather than aesthetics and forms of expression. The most prominent of the progressive writers was Faiz Ahmad Faiz, who succeeded in blending ideas and aesthetics in his poems.

Contact with Islamic culture, beginning in the early eighth century, brought a fusion of Indian and Muslim thought, as reflected in the *thumri* ("thoom-ri") and *ghazal* ("gheh-zehl"), or love poetry. The *ghazal* is a short poem made up of couplets, each a complete idea in itself. The first couplet sets the tone of the poem, and the last couplet usually expresses a personal thought or intent, such as a prayer for a loved one.

MUSIC

Classical Indian music is spiritual in character. Sound is believed to have originated as a divine gift of the Lord of all Creation, Brahma. From this mystical origin, classical Indian music developed into a complex system as early as the second century A.D. Temples served as places of learning and performing. Gods and goddesses provided the theme.

When Muslim rulers introduced music in their courts, romantic and secular music began to evolve with Persian and central Asian elements. This gave rise to two distinct styles of music: the northern Hindustani and the southern Karnatak.

Both styles are based on the system of *raga* ("rah-gah"), which means "color" or "mood." A *raga* is a melodic base with characteristic ascending and descending notes. It conveys a mood or an emotion. In fact, there is a *raga* for every occasion—even for every part of the day! The individual performer interprets a melody to produce hours of improvised music. This is what makes Indian music unique.

Indian music follows a rhythm cycle known as *tala* ("tah-lah"). Complex rhythmic patterns are woven in, and improvisation is allowed. In a classical music ensemble, a percussion instrument to mark the beat and a violin or a *sarangi* ("sah-REHNG-gi")—a string instrument played with a bow—provide the accompaniment.

Shehnai, a wind-pipe instrument, and drums.

There are no notations in Indian music. The *guru* teaches his students by oral demonstration, and much is learned through attentive listening and years of practice. Traditionally, students live with their *guru* and absorb the master's technique.

MUSICAL INSTRUMENTS

There are about 500 different kinds of Indian musical instruments, each with a distinct shape and tone. Many are indigenous, some are of foreign origin, and a few are ingenious adaptations. Most can be classified as string, wind, or percussion instruments.

The most ancient of these instruments are the drums and gongs. The name for the southern Indian percussion, *mridangam* (body of clay), suggests its primitive beginnings. The highly refined modern *mridangam* is capable of producing a wide variety of sounds. In the north, the tabla, a two-piece drum possibly derived from the Arabic tabla, constitutes a vital part of Indian music today.

String instruments are of the bowing, plucking, and striking kind. The simplest of all is the one-string *ektara* (drone) that the singing bards carry. The *veena*, popular in the south today, was prevalent even in King Asoka's time (third century B.C.).

The *sitar*, made popular by the famous classical music genius, Ravi Shankar, is derived from the Persian *sehtar* and adapted by the 13th-century court poet, Amir Khusrau. The sarod is evolved from Afghanistan's *rebab*, while the Western violin has found a permanent place among classic Indian instruments.

Wind instruments include the bamboo flute and the reed-piped *nadaswaram* and *shehnai*. None of these have metallic keys like their Western counterparts do. Clever manipulation of the stops or fingerholes is required.

Sarangi, a string instrument played with a bow, and a drum.

Kathak dancers perform a modern ballet.

CLASSICAL DANCE

Classical dance in India is based on standards laid down by the sage Bharatha more than 2,000 years ago. They pertain to footwork, gestures, facial expressions, dress, and makeup. Five regional styles have evolved based on these forms.

The southern *Bharathanatyam* ("bhah-rah-tah-NEHT-yehm") is one of the most popular forms. Dancers in elaborate costume, jewelry, and hairdos perform intricate footwork in a half-seated posture. Hand gestures and facial expressions narrate mythic, heroic, or romantic tales. One dancer enacts all the roles, switching from emotion to emotion—joy, anger, mirth, fear, anguish, sorrow, and so on.

Kathakali ("kehth-keh-li") is the mimetic or mime-like dance of Kerala. With huge headdresses and heavily painted faces, men enact supernatural roles, often both male and female. Powerful percussion instruments accompany this outdoor dance, usually performed in the temple courtyard.

Odissi ("oh-DIS-si"), the dance form of eastern India, is flowing and sensuous, reminding one of the beautiful sculptures of the Konarak temple in Orissa. *Manipuri* is another eastern dance, the subtle movements of which resemble Burmese, Thai, and Cambodian dances.

Kathak ("keh-thek") is the northern form, which emphasizes footwork and swift, swirling pirouettes. Having entered the royal courts of the Muslim kings in the medieval period, *Kathak* has assimilated other cultural influences. *Kuchipudi* and *Mohiniattam* are neoclassical dances of the south, with strong folk elements in their music and gestures.

Uday Shankar, Rukmini Devi, and Balasaraswati are three of the best-known Indian classical dancers.

Above: **Kathakali**, the mimetic dance-drama of Kerala.

Left: **A** Bharathanatyam dancer.

THEATER

Traditional Indian theater is more like a dance drama; it is very different from the dialogue-based Western drama. Rural regions have a whole array of folk forms such as musical opera, masked theater, and puppetry. Generally, in Indian theater, a narrator links up plots and subplots, and a clown provides humor in between. The rest of the cast is broadly classified as good or bad characters.

With a simple orchestra, a temporarily constructed wooden stage, and elaborate dress and makeup, actors and actresses entertain the villagers from dusk to dawn on festive occasions. Regional styles may vary, but the themes are generally from old world legends: the *Puranas*, the *Ramayana,* and the *Mahabharata.*

In the past, a whole social class of performers grew out of the theatrical tradition. Chakyars or Bhagavatars in the south, originally of the Brahmin caste, took to entertaining to teach the people moral values. The art of storytelling was taken up by *bhanas* ("bhah-nahs"), the singing minstrels. Only temple dancers, known as *devadasis* ("they-vah-thah-sees"), were considered socially inferior. The *devadasi* system was later outlawed because of exploitation by wealthy patrons.

Modern Indian plays are quite like plays performed on a western stage; mythical themes are replaced by social themes, and dialogue dominates the show. Mumbai and Bengal produce plays that are a blend of Western and Indian theater.

Unfortunately, movies and television are fast replacing the stage in many rural and urban places. But the *Ramayana* and the *Mahabharata* have made a dramatic comeback in the form of television serials—old themes in a new medium.

A colorful cast of Indian marionettes.

ARCHITECTURE

India is full of artistic legacies from the past. One of the most obvious is Indian architecture, which is a tapestry of buildings incorporating many art forms. Some are in total ruin, while others remain astonishingly intact. The southern Hindu temples are architectural masterpieces, and the Hoysala temples at Habebid in Mysore have been described as a "stone lace-work of moving magnificence."

Elura in Hyderabad boasts an architectural marvel. There, craftsmen once excavated huge mountain rocks, carved the walls into powerful pillars and statues, chiseled out the interior to fill it with amazing frescos, and then carved a series of chapels and monasteries deep into the rock. These are known as the Kailasa temple, the mountain abode of Lord Shiva.

A Jain saint decorates a niche in Gwalior, Madhya Pradesh. Some of the finest sculptures are found in such niches carved out of cliff walls.

The five-tier Qutb Minar was started in A.D. 1199 as a victory memorial.

In the medieval period, many temples in the north were razed to make way for mosques, minarets, and tombs. The 250-foot (76-m) Qutb Minar, the Jama Masjid or Pearl Mosque, and the tombs scattered all over the old city of Delhi testify to this transformation. Elsewhere, slender minarets and spired domes with intricate inlays are reminders of Indo-Muslim art.

The British gave India the imposing Gateway of India in Mumbai and the Victorian-style palace of the viceroy in New Delhi. Today, the latter is known as the Rashtrapathi Bhavan and serves as the residence of the president of India. Some of the universities, churches, and libraries in Mumbai, Chennai, and Calcutta were built during India's colonial era.

Buildings in Pondicherry are distinctly French in structure, while those in Goa, near Mumbai, display a strong Portuguese influence.

Left: **The Mysore Palace has stained glass windows and solid silver doors.**

Below: **The Red Fort of Old Delhi was built in 1565.**

LEISURE

LIFE MOVES AT A SLOW PACE IN INDIA—slower than in many other countries. Indians have plenty of time for recreation and entertainment, and those who live in the rural areas generally have more leisure time than those in the cities.

People in the countryside revel in outdoor games; indoor games such as chess, parcheesi, and five stones, a game of throwing and hopping five little stones; street shows and other traditional pastimes; and competitive games such as racing, wrestling, and *kabaddi* ("kah-bah-di"), a team game that requires skillful breathing and dodging.

In the cities, most of the games introduced by the British are popular. Generally, the Bengalis prefer soccer, the Punjabis prefer hockey, and the residents of Mumbai prefer cricket. In the mountainous regions, climbing, trekking, and skiing are seasonal sports, while in the coastal regions, swimming, fishing, and boat-racing are the obvious favorites.

In the world of entertainment, India is known for its traditional storytellers—the bardic folk singers of the north or the bhagavatars of the south—who weave tales with songs and mimicry, holding their listeners' attention for hours. Some of these storytellers even double as puppeteers to recreate myths and legends.

Above: **"Simon says, 'Hands up!'"**

Opposite: **A kite vendor. The kites look simple, but the thick spools of string attest to their capability.**

The movies—the modern storyteller in India.

STORYTELLING

The bhagavatars sing their tales in temples, infusing them with religious and moral values. The *Ramayana* and the *Mahabharata*, which highlight the triumph of the righteous over the wicked, are of eternal interest.

But the movie theater has become the most popular form of entertainment, and television has invaded even the most remote villages. Film heroes and heroines have cashed in on mass adulation, and some have even taken on new roles in politics.

THE RAMAYANA

Once there lived a king named Dasharatha, who had three wives and four sons. His eldest son, Rama, was exiled for 14 years, just when he was about to be crowned, because the king was bound by promises he had made to his youngest queen. When Rama was in the forest with his wife Sita and brother Lakshmana, a wicked and lustful king, Ravana, came in the guise of a sage and abducted Sita. Rama and Lakshmana, with the help of the monkey god Hanuman, went in search of Sita. They killed Ravana and his mighty army, and Rama returned to rule. In this tale, Rama stands for righteous duty, Sita for purity and truth, and Ravana for arrogance and greed. The *Ramayana* is a living tradition in India and other parts of Asia.

TRADITIONAL PASTIMES

Manufactured toys and games are few in rural communities; play is often the product of ingenuity and imagination. Many wooden and clay dolls in India resemble Hindu gods and goddesses, because they have been shaped by the same artisans who produce holy images for religious use.

Girls in India usually play jump rope, or hopscotch, and five stones, tossing the stones up in the air and catching them in many different ways. The swing is so popular in India that homes in the south have permanent swings installed in their yards. In the north, women celebrate a festival called Teej, when tall swings are set up amid groves of trees for young and old to swing in and sing praises of the monsoon season.

Indian girls playing five stones on a sidewalk.

Organized sporting events are usually a feature of festivals. In the colorful harvest festival of Onam in Kerala, in the months of August and September, beautifully decorated boat processions culminate in exciting snakeboat races, very similar to Chinese dragon boat races in Singapore and Hong Kong.

The harvest festivals of Tamil Nadu feature bullock races and bullfighting competitions, while camel races and polo take center stage in the desert festivals of Rajasthan. Then there are the coconut-plucking contests, groundnut-eating races, and even bride-winning feats of rural India. But at the top of the list is the traveling circus. Folks travel from the villages by the busload, when the circus comes to town.

GAMES FROM THE PAST

Since ancient times, Indians have been known to spend hours playing board games: archeological digs have unearthed stone and ivory dice. Gambling and bullfighting are believed to have been introduced in southern India by Roman seafarers, while archery and hunting were the preserve of royalty in Vedic times.

Chess is known to have originated in India, from where the game spread to West and Southeast Asia. The Malay tiger game has its origin in the southern Indian game of *puli kattu* ("poo-li kaht-too"), a board game played with three tigers to a dozen goats, represented by stones and shells. To score, the goats—represented by stones—must completely encircle each tiger—represented by a shell.

Parcheesi is a common indoor game in the villages. There is a parcheesi gameboard carved on the wall of the fifth-century-A.D. temple on Elephanta Island near Mumbai. The game was so popular with the Mughal Emperor Akbar that he ordered parcheesi squares to be cut in the pavement of his palace quadrangle and used his slaves as living pieces.

Akbar also introduced polo from Persia in northern India, from where the sport spread to England in the 19th century. Polo is still played in northwestern India and in the Himalayan regions.

Thanks to India's wildlife protection policy, tiger and lion hunting, popular in the medieval period, especially among the maharajas, has been replaced by a less cruel form of hunting—shooting with a camera.

KABADDI AND YOGA

Two outdoor games that are distinctly Indian and require considerable skill are *kabaddi* and *kho-kho*. *Kabaddi* requires neither elaborate equipment nor a sports arena. Any number of people, organized in two teams, can play this simple game of breath control.

A line is drawn on the ground, and the teams gather on either side. A player from one team runs into the opposing team's side. He shouts "kabaddi" or "hu-tu-tu" without stopping to breathe and tries to touch a member of the opposing team and run back to his own team before his breath runs out. The opposing team's members try to dodge the intruder. But if one of them is hit, they band together to try to keep the intruder away from his team. If the intruder manages to reunite with his team before running out of breath, his team scores a point. Otherwise, the opposing team scores.

A great part of the fun in *kabaddi* is crowd participation. Spectators cheer and jeer, and some bet heavily on the outcome as the match gathers momentum.

Kho-kho ("khoh-khoh"), a catching game played by two teams of girls, has also become one of India's national games.

Learning to control the mind and body is the object of yoga and the martial arts of *kalari payat* ("kah-lah-ri pah-yat"). Some schools teach yoga to help children build supple bodies and a sharp intellect. Health conscious city folk take morning walks and practice yoga in gardens and parks.

Opposite top: **Puli kattu.** Three tigers and 12 goats represented by shells and stones are moved around a roughly drawn surface.

Opposite bottom: **Hunting, a sport for some Indians, is serious work for others.**

Below: **Stretching exercises in the park are a refreshing workout for this group of senior citizens.**

111

Ski resorts are vacation destinations for the rich and fashionable.

MODERN SPORTS

India is progressing in the world of sports. Good facilities have been provided for sportsmen and sportswomen, games are promoted, and grants are awarded to the skilled and talented.

Soccer, field hockey, basketball, volleyball, and cricket are popular group sports in urban India. Elite clubs offer tennis, badminton, squash, golf, and billiards. Skiing, skating, vintage car rallies, and yachting are rising recreational activities among the affluent.

Closest to the heart for most Indians is cricket. When the national team plays test matches, ears tune in to radios blaring the running commentary. When the Indian team won a test match a few years ago, Chennai declared a holiday, and revelers took to the streets, singing, dancing, and setting off firecrackers.

India pioneered the Asian Games, held for the first time in New Delhi in March 1951. When the 11th Asian Games returned to India in 1982, more than 30 countries were represented by about 5,000 participants in the spectacular event.

Above: **Residents of an Indian suburb watching a match. Sports are as much for the spectators as for the players.**

Left: **Many Indians make good hockey players.**

FESTIVALS

FESTIVALS ARE A COLORFUL EXPRESSION of Indian traditions: of changing seasons and harvesting cycles, of Vedic myths and legends, of social and spiritual renewal.

Indian festivals are bewilderingly diverse. Most of them have a religious character, some being an interesting fusion of Hindu-Buddhist, Hindu-Muslim, or Hindu-Christian beliefs. Some are national, secular events, such as Republic Day (January 26) and Independence Day (August 31). Many are confined to specific regions and religions, while a few are celebrated only by certain castes and clans.

With more than six religions celebrating the birthdays of gods and saints, Indians have a multitude of occasions to celebrate. In fact, there is some social revelry or temple festivity almost every other day of the year. Hindu festival dates are fixed by the Indian calendar, which follows the lunar cycle and also corresponds with the agricultural cycle of sowing and reaping.

Festivals in the villages are invariably accompanied by fairs and cultural performances that may go on for a week to 10 days. Often, plants and animals too have a place in the celebrations, and on at least one occasion, even the spirits of the dead are invited. Hindu festivals often begin with fasting and end with feasting; disciplined abstinence is a prelude to joyous abandon.

Below: **Butterfly dancers in a street parade.**

Opposite: **Giant effigies erected for the festival of Dussehra.**

Buddhist monks wear ceremonial headdresses for a Ladakhi festival.

COMMON FESTIVALS

The New Year is celebrated in India sometime in the month of Chaitra (mid-March to mid-April). It is called Guḍi Padwa in Maharashtra, Nav Warih in Kashmir, and Varuda Pirappu in Tamil Nadu. The date and method of celebration vary from place to place. Usually, singing and dancing culminate in a visit to a temple.

The second lunar month (April–May), known as Vaisaka, Baisakhi, or Vesak, is auspicious to Hindus, Buddhists, and Sikhs. The full moon day of Vaisaka is associated with Buddha's birth, enlightenment, and *nirvana* (release from the cycle of births and deaths). Interestingly, the Hindus regard it as the birth star of Shiva's son, Kartikeyan, who also grants enlightenment to his worshipers on this day. Buddhists form a procession led by an image of Buddha riding a chariot drawn by four horses. The devotees go around the temple, prostrating themselves and chanting, offering prayers and lighting candles at the altar, releasing caged animals, and performing acts of charity.

The first new moon day of April–May is the birth anniversary of Guru Hargobind, the founder of the Sikh movement Khalsa. The Sikh New Year, known as Baisakhi, is primarily a social occasion when the traditional Bhangra is danced all through the night. Punjabi villagers dress colorfully, take part in processions, drink, and sing joyfully.

FAMILY FESTIVALS

Although there is no Father's Day, Mother's Day, or Senior Citizen's Day in India, there are many festivals that celebrate family relationships.

In the north, during the festival of Raksha Bandhan, a girl ties a decorated silk thread around her brother's wrist and applies a dot of vermilion powder on his forehead. She makes sweets for him as a symbol of her affection. Her brother in turn gives her gifts and promises to protect her all his life, thus strengthening the sibling bond.

A festival called Karva Chauth in the north and Karadaya Nonbu in the south is celebrated to strengthen affection between married couples. The wife prays for the husband's well-being and fasts for a day, at the end of which she is blessed with a happy married life.

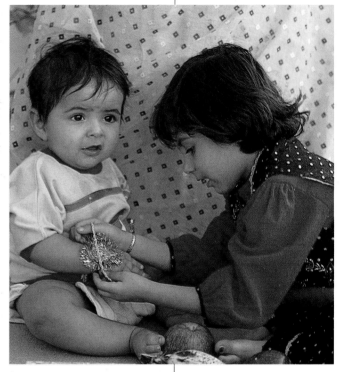

A girl ties a silk thread around her little brother's wrist during the festival of Raksha Bandhan.

Pitrupaksh or Shraddha is a ceremony devoted to ancestors. The spirits are believed to descend upon earth to participate in the ceremony sometime in the first two weeks of September. Food and prayers are offered to crows, who represent the spirits of the dead. Some Indians observe this ceremony on the death anniversary of their relatives.

At around the same time, Muslims celebrate Shab-e-Barat, a day when God is believed to register a person's actions and dispense his or her fate accordingly. It is an occasion for prayer, fasting, acts of charity, visits to family graves, and offerings of flowers, all of which is followed by feasting and merrymaking.

FESTIVAL MYTHS AND LEGENDS

Every Hindu festival is associated with a mythological tale. The northern festival of Raksha Bandhan recalls the legend of Lord Indra's defeat of the devil. When Indra was fighting a losing battle against the devil, his wife, Indrani, tied a sacred thread around his wrist. With the power of the thread, Indra won the battle.

Dussehra, called Durga Puja in Bengal, commemorates the defeat of a demon king by the goddess Durga. Legend has it that the buffalo-headed demon, Mahisasura, became insolent with power and brought pain and suffering on the pious and innocent. Angered by his arrogance, the Hindu Trinity, Brahman, created Durga, a deity with 1,000 arms. Mounted on a lion and armed with Shiva's trident, Vishnu's discus, and Brahma's thunderbolt, Durga conquered the demon.

In Bengal, huge images of Durga are installed in public places for nine days, and then carried by processions of devotees to rivers and lakes for immersion in the water. In Gujarat, women sing and dance the traditional Garba and Raas around images of the deity. In Uttar Pradesh and Delhi, the story of *Ramayana* is re-enacted in street performances, and on the 10th day, giant effigies of the 10-headed king, Ravana, and his brothers are burned, symbolizing the victory of righteousness.

In the south, the same festival is known as the Doll's Festival. Women arrange images of deities and dolls on a platform in their homes and invite their female friends over, giving them coconuts, betel leaves, turmeric, and vermilion powder as symbols of fertility and prosperity.

Figurines of Durga for sale in Calcutta.

CALENDAR OF FESTIVALS

Pongal	Jan	South	Harvest thanksgiving
Republic Day	Jan 26	Pan-India	National holiday
Basant Panchami	Jan/Feb	North	Spring festival
Desert Festival	Jan/Feb	Rajasthan	Jaisalmer (fort) festival
Shivaratri	Feb/Mar	Pan-India	Lord Shiva's night
Kahjuraho	Feb/Mar	Madhya Pradesh	Dance festival
Holi	Mar	North	Spring/color festival
Jamshed Navroz	Mar	Maharashtra	Parsi New Year
Gangaur	Mar/Apr	Rajasthan	Women's festival
Mahavir Jayanti	Mar/Apr	Pan-India	Jain festival
Easter	Mar/Apr	Pan-India	Christian festival
Varuda Pirappu	Apr	South	Tamil New Year
Meenakshi	Apr	Tamil Nadu	Goddess Meenakshi's marriage anniversary
Vaisaka	Apr/May	Pan-India	Buddhist festival
Baisakhi	Apr/May	North	Sikh New Year
Pooram	Apr/May	Kerala	Hindu temple festival
Eid-ul-Fitr	May	Pan-India	Muslim festival
Hemis festival	Jun/Jul	Ladakh, Jammu, Kashmir	Buddhist festival
Rath Yatra	Jul	Orissa	Hindu temple festival
Naag Panchami	Jul/Aug	Pan-India	Snake festival
Raksha Bandhan	Jul/Aug	North	Brother's Day
Amarnath	Jul/Aug	Kashmir	Lord Shiva festival
Teej	Jul/Aug	Rajasthan	Swing festival
Independence Day	Aug 15	Pan-India	National holiday
Onam	Aug/Sep	Kerala	Boat festival
Janmashtami	Aug/Sep	Pan-India	Lord Krishna's birthday
Eid-ul-Azha	Aug/Sep	Pan-India	Muslim festival
Ganesh Chathurthi	Aug/Sep	Pan-India	Ganesha festival
Dussehra	Sep/Oct	Pan-India	Durga/Rama festival
Muharram	Oct	Pan-India	Muslim festival
Guru Purab	Oct/Nov	North	Guru Nanak's birthday
Diwali	Nov	Pan-India	Festival of lights
Christmas	Dec 25	Pan-India	Christian festival

"Lead me from the unreal to the real.
"Lead me from the darkness to light.
"Lead me from death to immortality."

—*An invocation from the Upanishads, the last part of the Vedas.*

DEEPAVALI AND HOLI

Diwali or Deepavali, the festival of lights, is India's most popular festival. It is believed that Lord Krishna killed the demon king, Narakasura, on this dark night. According to another belief, Diwali celebrates Lakshmi, the goddess of wealth and prosperity, who blesses the home and offices of her devotees on this auspicious day. Whichever the legend, it is a day when the whole of India unrestrainedly rejoices.

Homes, shops, and buildings are spring-cleaned and beautifully decorated with rows of lamps and candles. Several days prior to the festival, people start making sweet dishes and buying new clothes and jewelry for the occasion. Fireworks are the main attraction for children and adults alike. Many devotees visit the temple, and the young seek the blessings of the elders.

The spring festival of the north, popularly known as Holi, is also replete with color, fun, and gaiety. According to legend, Holika, the wicked aunt of the divine child Prahlada, decided to burn the boy as punishment for uttering the name of God in vain. Amazingly enough, the fire protected the child and burned his cruel aunt instead!

Huge bonfires are lit on the eve of Holi to mark the destruction of evil. Since Holi is also the water sport played by Lord Krishna and his milkmaids, the streets are full of people throwing colored water and powder at each other with glee. People also visit friends and eat lots of sweets.

Fireworks during the festival of Deepavali.

GODS' AND SAINTS' BIRTHDAYS

India celebrates the birthdays of gods, saints, *gurus*, and prophets grandly. In the villages, even local heroes receive honor fit for the gods.

Rama's birthday is a grand affair in temples dedicated to him, but it takes on a special significance in his birthplace, Ayodhya. On Krishna's birthday, vignettes from his life unfold in homes, temples, and cultural centers, and children dress up as Krishna and indulge in the naughty acts described in legendary tales of the god's childhood.

Christians celebrate the birth of Jesus Christ. They flock to church at midnight on Christmas Eve or on Christmas morning to attend mass and see a re-enactment of the nativity. In the cities, even the non-Christians put up Christmas trees, exchange gifts, and hold Christmas parties.

Muslims gather at mosques on Prophet Mohammed's birthday, Milad-un-Nabi, in the third month of the Islamic calendar. This day is marked by special religious discourses and the distribution of alms to the poor.

Sikhs celebrate Guru Purab to mark the birthday of their founder, Guru Nanak. Jains flock to the ancient Jain shrine at Girnar in Gujarat on Mahavira's birthday. Parsis celebrate Khordad Saal, the prophet Zoroaster's birthday, in their temples.

VILLAGE FAIRS

Fairs are an integral part of festivities in India, whatever the sect or religion. Residents of neighboring villages, dressed in all their finery, arrive at village fairs on camels, in bullock carts, on bicycles, and on foot. Hectic buying, bargaining, and selling are the order of the day. Things ranging from kitchen utensils, trinkets, and fresh vegetables to cows and horses are bought and sold. It is also the ideal time for selecting brides and grooms! Magic shows, street dances, puppet theater, folk music, circus shows, and impromptu acts add to the festive spirit of these fairs.

Elephant rides and camel races are common at the Teej and Pushkar fairs in Rajasthan. Bullfighting is a regular feature on the day following the harvest festival of Pongal (mid-January) in the south. Cockfights, and the accompanying heavy betting, are also common then. Boat races are popular with the seafarers and fishermen of Kerala during the festival of Onam.

In mountainous Ladakh, the annual fair at the beginning of spring includes a ritual performance in Buddhist monasteries. The actors and musicians are lamas or monks, who blow huge trumpets, clap cymbals, and beat drums. Masked figures, gorgeously attired in silk robes, represent spirits and demons. The victory of good and the defeat of the demons are re-enacted with stunning effect.

Jains hold an Arathyatra fair in Meerut in the north to celebrate the birth of three of their saints, called Tirthankaras. The full moon day in October–November sees more than a million Jains flocking to the fair.

Rides on elephants and ferris wheels are part of the fun at festival fairs.

TESTS OF FAITH

Firewalking is a common test of faith in many rural communities in India. Once a year in the south, firewalking serves as a wish-fulfilling ritual performed in honor of local deities or to ensure a good harvest. Brave Hindu youths bathe in the temple complex, smear their bodies with turmeric, and walk over a bed of live coals.

Muslims, especially the Shias, commemorate the martyrdom of Imam Husain, the grandson of Prophet Mohammed, with a month of fasting and prayers. Known as Muharram, the first month of the Islamic calendar is a solemn period observed with great fervor especially in Lucknow, where, watched by thousands, bands of men walk on beds of live coals. Some even lash themselves with whips in a show of grief.

The Goan festival Zatra celebrates the visit of the three kings to Bethlehem, where Christ was born. Three young men dressed as the three kings walk up to a church that shelters a sculpture of the Holy Infant Jesus. The actors' entrance into the church kicks off feasting and dancing, firewalking and fire-eating.

In January, pious devotees of the god Aiyappa abstain from meat, alcohol, and sex, impose other forms of severe discipline on themselves, and walk barefoot several miles up the hill of Sabri Malai in the south.

Firewalking is a test of faith and sometimes the fulfillment of a vow.

FOOD

"YOU ARE WHAT YOU EAT," especially in India, where food is considered as sacred as the human body. Indians look for balanced nourishment of both body and mind, in the belief that what they eat influences their behavior, attitudes, and well-being.

Spices, milk and milk products, meat, lentils, and vegetables are used in varying amounts, depending on the season, month, or day. All foods have been classified by an ancient science into heating and cooling agents. Indians believe, for instance, that mangoes produce heat, while milk and yogurt cool the body. Children are generally given a glass of milk after they eat mangoes to prevent boils and sores in the heat of summer—and it seems to work!

Each food item is believed to possess certain qualities that are transmitted to the consumer. Meat, alcohol, and highly fermented foods are considered base foods that contribute to laziness and greed. Rich and oily foods, having excess spice or sugar, are considered royal foods that produce a quick temper and a love of luxury. Indians who wish to calm the body and sharpen the mind should live on a diet of milk and milk products, fresh fruits and vegetables, lentils, nuts, and cereals.

Such food values have considerably influenced the daily diet and eating habits of most Indians.

Left and below: **Fruit stands can be seen almost everywhere in India.**

Opposite: **A bare glimpse of India's colorful cuisine.**

A variety of lentils, spices, and other dried foods used in Indian cooking.

FOOD VARIETIES

Indian cuisine is as rich and colorful as the country itself. Every region has its own food specialties, although there is a standard Indian meal, consisting of vegetables, meat or fish, a cereal, some yogurt, and lentils, or *dhal* ("dhahl").

Depending on the region, the cereal could be rice or an Indian wheat bread, such as *chapati* ("cheh-PAH-ti"), *puri* ("POO-ri"), *naan* ("nahn"), or *paratha* ("peh-RAH-thah"). In many middle-class homes, both *chapati* and rice, often spiced and garnished with vegetables and nuts, are served. But a poor man's diet might only consist of rice porridge or plain bread with raw onions and green chili.

Lentils are a major source of protein for Indians, and India produces a wide variety of split peas and beans. Lentils are generally eaten daily, and many spices are used to create a range of flavored lentil dishes.

Vegetables in season, including gourds, greens, and root vegetables, are popular throughout India. Banana curries and pumpkin with a liberal dash of freshly grated coconut are typical in the south, while a dish of green peppers and cauliflower in onion, garlic, and tomato sauce is popular in the north.

Egg and chicken are commonly eaten throughout India; fish and shrimp are hot favorites in the coastal regions.

Islamic influence shows in royal Mughal-style recipes. The conical earthen oven called *tandoor* ("tehn-dur") has added a spread of oven-baked *tandoori* breads, such as *naan*, and *tandoori* meats, such as chicken and mutton, to the Indian menu.

LAMB AND CASHEW NUT CURRY

This is a northern Indian dish, usually served with a long-grained rice (preferably Basmati rice, available at Asian groceries).

1½-inch (3.8-cm) piece of fresh, peeled ginger
3 cloves garlic
2 green chili peppers
¼ tsp cardamon seeds, removed from pod (available at Asian groceries)
1½ oz unsalted cashew nuts (24–35 nuts)
1½ tbsp ground coriander
1 tsp ground turmeric
1 tsp chili powder
⅛ tsp ground cloves
3 tbsp ghee (available at Asian groceries), or cooking oil
2 onions, finely chopped
2¼ lbs lamb, cut into bite-sized pieces
½ cup plain yogurt
¾ cup water
1½ tsp sugar
1¼ tsp salt
½ tbsp lime or lemon juice
1 tbsp cilantro (also called Chinese parsley or coriander leaves), finely
    chopped

In a blender, grind the ginger, garlic, green chili peppers, cardamon seeds, and cashew nuts into a smooth paste. Add the ground spices (coriander, turmeric, chili powder, and cloves) to the paste and mix well. Set aside.

Heat the ghee or oil in a Dutch oven. When the oil is warm, add the onions and saute until golden brown. Stir in the blended ingredients and saute for about three minutes, stirring constantly. Add the lamb; at this point the temperature should be sufficiently high to brown the meat all over. When the lamb is well sealed, blend in the yogurt, water, sugar, and salt, in that order. Bring to a boil, reduce to low heat, and simmer for an hour. Add the lemon juice and coriander leaves and simmer for an additional 20 minutes or until the lamb is tender.

Beef or chicken may be substituted for lamb, if desired. For chicken, use only half a cup of water.

HABITS AND PRACTICES

Generally, Indians rinse their hands, legs, and face before a meal, at which they sit on the floor and eat with their fingers. Among Hindus, food is first offered to the gods and then served to the family by the woman of the house, who eats only when everyone else has finished.

Indians usually use stainless steel or brass vessels and plates. The wealthy use silver plates; the poorer place their food portions on rectangular sections of banana leaves. In many urban homes, partakers of a meal sit at a dining table and use Western-style cutlery.

A traditional Bengali meal takes hours to prepare and is consumed at a leisurely pace. Each person sits on a small carpet on the floor. A large steel platter or piece of fresh-cut banana leaf lying in front of the carpet presents hot rice with lime wedges, whole green chilies, and a little pickle. Small metal or earthen bowls around the platter contain portions of dahl, vegetables, fish, meat, and yogurt.

Wasting food is considered sinful among Indians. Children are told that wasted food goes to the Ganges River to cry. In the villages, leftovers are given to animals; in the cities, to servants and street beggars.

Eating times vary from region to region. Southern Indians generally do not eat breakfast, but have a very early brunch. Bengalis are known to have dinner very late at night.

An Indian wedding feast.

128

TABOOS AND PREFERENCES

Abstinence from food and drink is part and parcel of Indian life. One may fast temporarily or avoid particular foods or both. Most Indians avoid meat on occasion, and many are vegetarian for life. Beef, to Hindus, and pork, to Muslims, are forbidden foods. Muslims eat only *halal* foods, that is, meat and other edible products made from animals that have been slaughtered in the Islamic way.

Brahmins, some of the Hindu merchant communities, Jains, and many Buddhists are strict lacto-vegetarians. They consume milk products, but avoid eggs, fish, chicken, and meat. Orthodox Brahmins and Jains avoid onions, garlic, coffee, and tea, as all these are believed to activate the baser passions. Strict food habits and a disciplined diet are considered essential for a spiritual life.

NAAN

Baked leavened bread, eaten with a lentil soup, a few meats and vegetables, and some yogurt.

2 cups (473 ml) all-purpose flour
$\frac{1}{2}$ teaspoon baking powder
1 teaspoon salt
1 teaspoon sugar
1 teaspoon active dry yeast

$\frac{2}{3}$ cup (158 ml) milk
$\frac{2}{3}$ cup (158 ml) unflavored yogurt
1 egg, beaten
2 teaspoons poppy seeds (optional)

Sift flour, baking powder, salt, and sugar in a bowl. Mix yeast and a little milk into a paste. Beat yogurt with remaining milk and heat until lukewarm. Stir in yeast paste. Add yogurt and yeast mixture gradually to flour and knead into a dough. Add egg and knead again. Cover dough with a damp cloth and leave in a warm place for $1\frac{1}{2}$ hours or until doubled in size. Break dough into 6–8 pieces. Roll into balls and flatten with your hands. Press poppy seeds (if using) into bread with your fingers. Bake bread in preheated oven at 450°F (230°C) for 12 minutes or until puffed and blistered. Serve hot.

RASGULLA

Cream cheese balls in syrup.

$2^{1}/_{2}$ cups (591 ml) milk
1 cup (237 ml) unflavored yogurt
2 teaspoons lemon juice
$1^{1}/_{2}$ teaspoons salt
$^{3}/_{4}$ cup (177 ml) chopped almonds

$^{2}/_{3}$ cup (158 ml) semolina flour
$3^{3}/_{4}$ cups (887 ml) water
4 cups (946 ml) sugar
pinch of cream of tartar
$^{1}/_{2}$ teaspoon rose water

Boil milk and add yogurt, lemon juice, and salt. Leave for 12 hours at approximately 98°F (37°C). Strain curdled mixture through a clean piece of cheesecloth until almost dry. Wrap cloth around cheese and place under a heavy weight. Leave to drain for 3 hours. Add almonds and semolina flour and knead into a soft dough. Break dough into 12–15 small balls and set aside. Boil water, sugar, and cream of tartar until sugar dissolves. Carefully drop dough balls into syrup and simmer gently for 2 hours. Stir in rose water. Serve hot or cold.

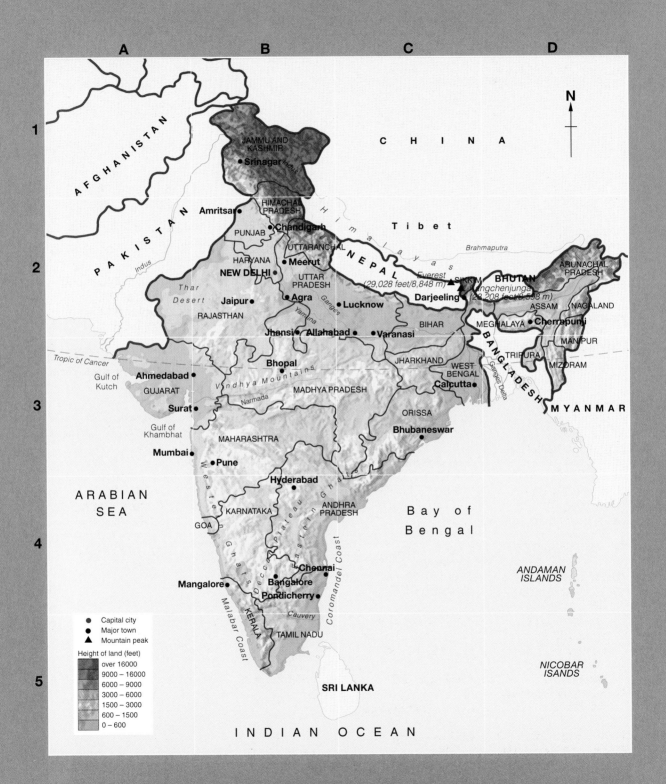

A B C D

1

AFGHANISTAN

PAKISTAN

JAMMU AND
KASHMIR
• Srinagar

CHINA

Tibet

Himalayas

Brahmaputra

HIMACHAL
PRADESH

2

Amritsar•

PUNJAB

•Chandigarh

UTTARANCHAL

NEPAL

Everest
(29,028 feet/8,848 m)

SIKKIM

BHUTAN
Kngchenjunga
(28,208 feet/8,598 m)

ARUNACHAL
PRADESH

HARYANA

•Meerut

NEW DELHI

UTTAR
PRADESH

Thar
Desert

Jaipur•

RAJASTHAN

•Agra

Ganges

•Lucknow

Darjeeling•

ASSAM

NAGALAND

Yamuna

Jhansi•

•Allahabad•

•Varanasi

BIHAR

MEGHALAYA

•Cherrapunji

MANIPUR

BANGLADESH

TRIPURA

MIZORAM

Tropic of Cancer

Bhopal•

Vindhya Mountains

JHARKHAND

Gulf of
Kutch

Ahmedabad•

GUJARAT

Narmada

MADHYA PRADESH

WEST
BENGAL

•Calcutta

Ganges Delta

MYANMAR

3

Surat•

Gulf of
Khambhat

ORISSA

•Bhubaneswar

MAHARASHTRA

Mumbai•

•Pune

Western Ghats

ARABIAN
SEA

Hyderabad•

Deccan Plateau

Eastern Ghats

ANDHRA
PRADESH

Bay of
Bengal

ANDAMAN
ISLANDS

KARNATAKA

GOA

4

Mangalore•

KERALA

Malabar Coast

•Bangalore
Pondicherry•

•Chennai

Cauvery

Coromandel Coast

NICOBAR
ISANDS

Capital city
Major town
▲ Mountain peak

Height of land (feet)
over 16000
9000 – 16000
6000 – 9000
3000 – 6000
1500 – 3000
600 – 1500
0 – 600

TAMIL NADU

5

SRI LANKA

INDIAN OCEAN

N

MAP OF INDIA

ECONOMIC INDIA

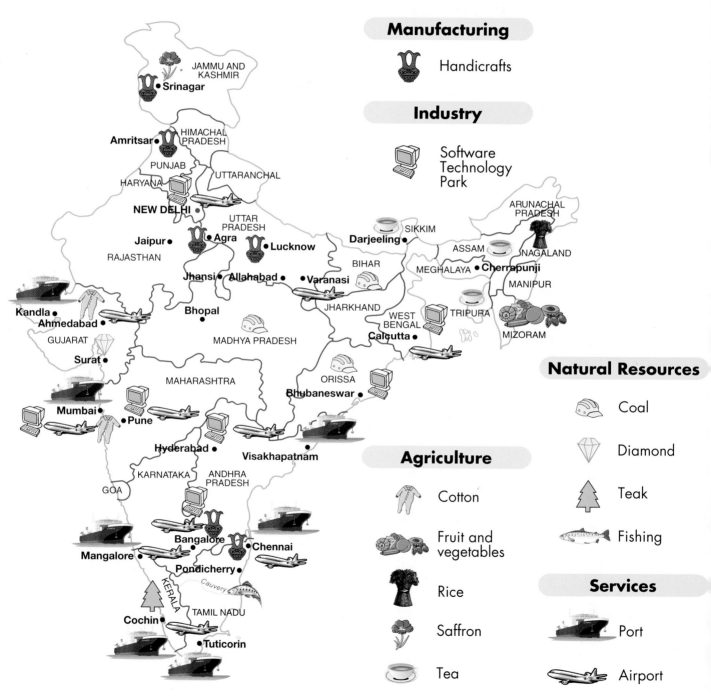

Manufacturing
Handicrafts

Industry
Software Technology Park

Agriculture
Cotton

Fruit and vegetables

Rice

Saffron

Tea

Natural Resources
Coal

Diamond

Teak

Fishing

Services
Port

Airport

JAMMU AND KASHMIR
Srinagar

Amritsar
HIMACHAL PRADESH
PUNJAB
UTTARANCHAL
HARYANA
NEW DELHI

Jaipur
RAJASTHAN
Agra
UTTAR PRADESH
Lucknow

Jhansi
Allahabad
Varanasi
BIHAR

Darjeeling
SIKKIM
ARUNACHAL PRADESH
ASSAM
NAGALAND

MEGHALAYA
Cherrapunji
MANIPUR

Bhopal
JHARKHAND
WEST BENGAL
Calcutta
TRIPURA
MIZORAM

Kandla
Ahmedabad
GUJARAT
MADHYA PRADESH

Surat

MAHARASHTRA
ORISSA
Bhubaneswar

Mumbai
Pune
Hyderabad
Visakhapatnam

KARNATAKA
ANDHRA PRADESH
GOA

Bangalore
Chennai
Mangalore
Pondicherry
KERALA
Cauvery
TAMIL NADU
Cochin
Tuticorin

ABOUT THE ECONOMY

GROSS DOMESTIC PRODUCT (GDP)
US$1.7 trillion

GDP SECTORS
Agriculture 29.1%, industry and commerce 36.8%, public services 12.7%, transportation and communications 21.3% (1999–2000)

AGRICULTURAL PRODUCTS
Rice, wheat, oilseed, cotton, jute, tea, coffee, sugarcane, and potatoes; cattle, buffalo, sheep, goats, fish, and poultry

WORKFORCE
306 million (est.)

EMPLOYMENT PROFILE
Agriculture 67%, industry and commerce 19%, service and government 8%, transport and communications 3% (1995)

INFLATION
3 percent (1999–2000)

EXTERNAL DEBT
US$76 billion (1999–2000)

CURRENCY
1 Indian rupee (Re, plural Rs) = 100 paise
US$1 = 46 Rs (Feb 20, 2001)

POVERTY LEVEL
27 percent (2000)

NATURAL RESOURCES
Coal (fourth largest reserves in the world), iron ore, manganese, mica, bauxite, titanium ore, chromite, natural gas, diamonds, petroleum, limestone, and arable land

PORTS & HARBORS
Calcutta, Chennai, Cochin, Haldia, Kandla, Marmugao, Mumbai, Mangalore, Paradip, Tuticorin, Visakhapatnam

EXPORT PROCESSING ZONES
Calcutta, Chennai, Cochin, Kandla, Mumbai, Noida, and Visakhapatnam

SOFTWARE TECHNOLOGY PARKS
Bangalore, Thiruvananthapuram, Calcutta, Gandhinagar, Hyderabad, Jaipur, Mohali, Mumbai, Noida, Pune, and Bhubaneswar

MAJOR IMPORTS
Crude oil and petroleum products, machinery, gems, fertilizers, and chemicals

MAJOR EXPORTS
Agricultural produce, textiles, jute, chemicals, leather goods, iron, steel, precious stones

TRADING PARTNERS
United States, Hong Kong, United Kingdom, Japan, Germany, Belgium, and Saudi Arabia

CULTURAL INDIA

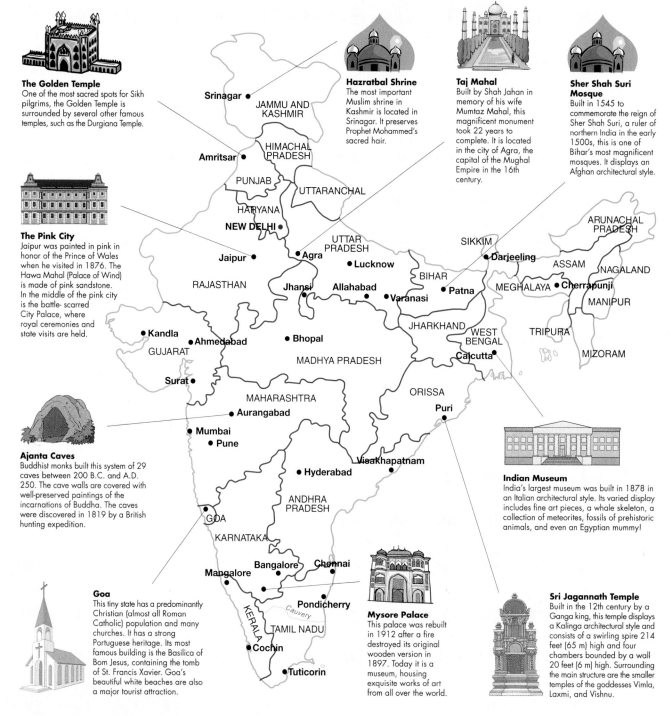

The Golden Temple
One of the most sacred spots for Sikh pilgrims, the Golden Temple is surrounded by several other famous temples, such as the Durgiana Temple.

Hazratbal Shrine
The most important Muslim shrine in Kashmir is located in Srinagar. It preserves Prophet Mohammed's sacred hair.

Taj Mahal
Built by Shah Jahan in memory of his wife Mumtaz Mahal, this magnificent monument took 22 years to complete. It is located in the city of Agra, the capital of the Mughal Empire in the 16th century.

Sher Shah Suri Mosque
Built in 1545 to commemorate the reign of Sher Shah Suri, a ruler of northern India in the early 1500s, this is one of Bihar's most magnificent mosques. It displays an Afghan architectural style.

The Pink City
Jaipur was painted in pink in honor of the Prince of Wales when he visited in 1876. The Hawa Mahal (Palace of Wind) is made of pink sandstone. In the middle of the pink city is the battle-scarred City Palace, where royal ceremonies and state visits are held.

Ajanta Caves
Buddhist monks built this system of 29 caves between 200 B.C. and A.D. 250. The cave walls are covered with well-preserved paintings of the incarnations of Buddha. The caves were discovered in 1819 by a British hunting expedition.

Indian Museum
India's largest museum was built in 1878 in an Italian architectural style. Its varied display includes fine art pieces, a whale skeleton, a collection of meteorites, fossils of prehistoric animals, and even an Egyptian mummy!

Goa
This tiny state has a predominantly Christian (almost all Roman Catholic) population and many churches. It has a strong Portuguese heritage. Its most famous building is the Basilica of Bom Jesus, containing the tomb of St. Francis Xavier. Goa's beautiful white beaches are also a major tourist attraction.

Mysore Palace
This palace was rebuilt in 1912 after a fire destroyed its original wooden version in 1897. Today it is a museum, housing exquisite works of art from all over the world.

Sri Jagannath Temple
Built in the 12th century by a Ganga king, this temple displays a Kalinga architectural style and consists of a swirling spire 214 feet (65 m) high and four chambers bounded by a wall 20 feet (6 m) high. Surrounding the main structure are the smaller temples of the goddesses Vimla, Laxmi, and Vishnu.

Map labels

Srinagar

JAMMU AND KASHMIR

HIMACHAL PRADESH

Amritsar

PUNJAB

UTTARANCHAL

HARYANA

NEW DELHI

Jaipur

RAJASTHAN

Jhansi

Agra

Lucknow

UTTAR PRADESH

Allahabad

Varanasi

BIHAR

Patna

SIKKIM

Darjeeling

ARUNACHAL PRADESH

ASSAM

NAGALAND

MEGHALAYA

Cherrapunji

MANIPUR

TRIPURA

MIZORAM

JHARKHAND

WEST BENGAL

Calcutta

Kandla

Ahmedabad

GUJARAT

Bhopal

MADHYA PRADESH

Surat

MAHARASHTRA

Aurangabad

Mumbai

Pune

ORISSA

Puri

Visakhapatnam

Hyderabad

ANDHRA PRADESH

GOA

KARNATAKA

Mangalore

Bangalore

Chennai

Pondicherry

Cauvery

KERALA

TAMIL NADU

Cochin

Tuticorin

ABOUT THE CULTURE

OFFICIAL NAME
Republic of India

CAPITAL
New Delhi

STATES
Andhra Pradesh, Arunachal Pradesh, Assam, Bihar, Goa, Gujarat, Haryana, Himachal Pradesh, Jammu and Kashmir, Karnataka, Kerala, Madhya Pradesh, Maharashtra, Manipur, Meghalaya, Mizoram, Nagaland, Orissa, Punjab, Rajasthan, Sikkim, Tamil Nadu, Tripura, Uttar Pradesh, and West Bengal

POPULATION
1,027,015,247 (Mar 1, 2001)

LIFE EXPECTANCY
61 years

OFFICIAL LANGUAGES
National: English and Hindi
State: Assamese, Bengali, Gujarati, Kannada, Kashmiri, Malayalam, Marathi, Oriya, Punjabi, Sanskrit, Sindhi, Tamil, Telugu, and Urdu

MAIN ETHNIC GROUPS
72% Indo-Aryan and 25% Dravidian

RELIGIONS
Hinduism, Islam, Christianity, Sikhism, and Buddhism

LITERACY RATE
52 percent

NATIONAL EMBLEM
Four lions rest on a circular abacus girded by four smaller animals: a lion, an elephant, a horse, and a bull. The abacus rests on a lotus in full bloom. The motto, Satyameva Jayate, means "Truth alone triumphs."

NATIONAL FLOWER
The Lotus or the Water Lily

HOLIDAYS & FESTIVALS
Desert Festival, Gangaur (Gauri, Goddess of Abundance), Holi Festival of Springtime, Ganesh Chaturthi (Ganesh, Elephant God), Diwali, Ladakh, Chaitra Parva Spring Festival, and Dussehra (triumph of Lord Rama over the demon Ravana)

IMPORTANT ANNIVERSARIES
Republic Day (Jan 26) and Independence Day (Aug 15)

LEADERS IN POLITICS
Mohandas Karamchand Gandhi, better known as Mahatma—peaceful independence fighter
Jawaharlal Nehru—first prime minister
Indira Gandhi—first woman prime minister
Atal Behari Vajpayee—current prime minister

TIME LINE

IN INDIA	IN THE WORLD
	753 B.C. Rome founded
327 B.C. Alexander the Great invades India.	
326-184 B.C. Mauryan Empire; Buddhism spreads.	
180 B.C. – A.D. 150 Saka era in Indus Valley.	**116–17 B.C.** Roman Empire reaches its greatest extent, under Emperor Trajan (98–17 B.C.).
	A.D. 600 Height of Mayan civilization
985 Rise of the Chola Dynasty.	**1000** Chinese perfect gunpowder and begin to use it in warfare.
1288 Marco Polo comes to India.	
1498 Vasco da Gama arrives in India.	
1510 Portuguese forces capture Goa.	**1530** Beginning of trans-Atlantic slave trade organized by Portuguese in Africa
	1558 – 1603 Reign of Elizabeth I of England
1600 British Crown grants charter to form East India Company.	**1620** Pilgrim Fathers sail the Mayflower to America
1631 Construction of the Taj Mahal.	
1686 English war with the Mughals.	
1757 Battle of Plassey in Bengal; British rule in India begins.	**1776** U. S. Declaration of Independence
	1789 – 1799 The French Revolution

IN INDIA	IN THE WORLD
1858 East India Company dissolves; Mughal Empire ends.	
1867 Mohandas Karamchand Gandhi is born.	**1861** U. S. Civil War begins.
1885 The Indian National Congress forms.	**1869** The Suez Canal is opened.
1905 Bengal partitions into East and West.	
	1914 World War I begins.
	1939 World War II begins.
	1945 The United States drops atomic bombs on Hiroshima and Nagasaki.
1947 India gains independence; Jawaharlal Nehru is first Prime minister. War with Pakistan.	
1948 Mahatma Gandhi is assassinated.	**1949** North Atlantic Treaty Organization (NATO) formed
	1957 Russians launch Sputnik.
1965 Second war with Pakistan.	**1966 – 1969** Chinese Cultural Revolution
1971 Third war with Pakistan.	
1984 Prime Minister Indira Gandhi is assassinated.	**1986** Nuclear power disaster at Chernobyl in Ukraine
1991 Former Prime Minister Rajiv Gandhi is assassinated. P.V. Narasimha Rao is elected India's ninth prime minister.	**1991** Break-up of Soviet Union
1996 Atal Behari Vajpayee becomes prime minister; he resigns after 13 days in office.	
1997 Kicheril Raman Narayanan is made president.	**1997** Hong Kong is returned to China.
1998 Vajpayee returns as prime minister.	**2001** World population surpasses 6 billion.

GLOSSARY

Aryan
Indian race of mixed origin; Indo-European.

burqah ("BUR-kah")
Head-to-toe veil worn by traditional Muslim women.

caste
Social class, originally based on occupation. Examples are the Brahmins (priests), Vaishyas (merchants), and Sudras (laborers).

Dravidian
Indigenous Indian ethnicity.

gotra ("go-trah")
One's ancestral lineage.

Hanafi
One of four teachings of the Sunni sect.

harijan ("hah-ri-jahn")
Children of god. The name given by Mahatma Gandhi to the "out-castes" known as the untouchables.

Hindu Trinity
Brahma the creator, Vishnu the preserver, and Shiva the destroyer.

jati ("jah-ti")
A clan.

kangri ("KAHNG-gree")
An earthen pot of hot coal used by Kashmiris to keep warm in winter.

karma ("kahr-mah")
A fundamental Hindu and Buddhist belief similar to the principle of cause and effect.

maharaja ("mah-hah-RAH-jah")
An Indian prince.

maulvi ("mole-vee")
Muslim priest.

moksha ("mohk-shah")
Hindu equivalent of the Buddhist *nirvana*—the release of the soul from the life cycle.

panchayats ("PEHN-chah-yehts")
Village and district courts.

satyagraha ("SEHT-yah-grah-hah")
The nonviolent fight for justice advocated by Mahatma Gandhi.

Sunni law
Islamic law based on the word of Prophet Mohammed, but not attributed to him.

Taj Mahal
The magnificent marble mausoleum in the city of Agra known as the eighth wonder of the world.

Vedas
Books of Knowledge. Sacred writings composed around 1500 BC. Mainly *Rig Veda, Sama Veda, Atharva Veda, Yajur Veda, Brahmanas*, and *Upanishads. Veda* means "knowledge" in Sanskrit.

FURTHER INFORMATION

BOOKS

Bond, Ruskin. *Children's Omnibus*. Delhi: Rupa Pub, 1995.

Bradnock, Robert and Roma Bradnock. *Footprint India Handbook 2001*. Illinois: Passport Books, 2001.

Das, Gurcharan. *India Unbound*. London: Knopf, 2001.

Davis, Richard. *Lives of Indian Images*. Delhi: Motilal Banarsidas Pub, 1999.

Freeman, James M. *Untouchable: An Indian Life History*. California: Stanford University Press, 1982.

Jafa, Jyoti. *Really, Your Highness*. Delhi: Roli Books, 2000.

Narayan, R.K. *The Indian Epics Retold*. London: Penguin Books, 2000.

Niven, Christine, et. al. Lonely Planet India. California: Lonely Planet Publications, 1999.

Seth, Vikram. *Beastly Tales from Here and There*. London: Viking/Penguin, 1999.

Seth, Vikram. *A Suitable Boy*. London: Penguin Books, 1999.

Treasury of Indian Tales. Delhi: Children's Book Trust, 1993.

Wolpert, Stanley A. *Gandhi's Passion: The Life and Legacy of Mahatma Gandhi*. Oxford: Oxford University Press, 2001.

WEBSITES

Central Intelligence Agency World Factbook (select India from the country list).
www.odci.gov/cia/publications/factbook/index.html

India Parliament Homepage. http://alfa.nic.in/

Indiabynet.com. www.indiabynet.com

Internet Indian History Sourcebook. www.fordham.edu/halsall/india/indiasbook.html

Lonely Planet World Guide: Destination India.
www.lonelyplanet.com/destinations/indian_subcontinent/india/

MapsofIndia.com. www.mapsofindia.com

The World Bank Group (type "India" in the search box). www.worldbank.org

The World-Wide Web Virtual Library: India. www.webhead.com/wwwvl/india/

CD-ROM/MUSIC

Hindi Guru. Magic Software. Released 1998.

Ravi Shankar Collection. Richard Bock and EMI Records. Released 1999.

Shree Ganesh: An auspicious beginning. Munsai Multimedia. Released 1999.

Three Best CD-ROMs from Amar Chitra Katha. Pheonix Global. Released 1998.

Vedic Presents Rhythmic Intelligence. Sub Rosa Records. Released 1997.

BIBLIOGRAPHY

Cummings, David. *India*. New York: Bookwright Press, 1989.

Das, Prodeepta. *Inside India*. New York: Franklin Watts, 1990.

Haskins, James. *Count Your Way Through India*. Minneapolis: Carolrhoda Books, 1990.

India in Pictures. Minneapolis: Lerner Publications, 1989.

McNair, Sylvia. *India*. Chicago: Children's Press, 1990.

Moon, Bernice and Cliff. *India is My Country*. New York: Marshall Cavendish, 1986.

Sarin, Amita Vohra. *India: An Ancient Land, A New Nation*. Minneapolis: Dillon Press, 1985.

Stewart, Gail. *India*. New York: Maxwell Macmillan International, 1992.

INDEX